The Complete Secrets of Happy Children

STEVE BIDDULPH
AND SHARON BIDDULPH

The Complete Secrets of Happy Children

Thorsons
CLASSICS

Thorsons
An imprint of HarperCollins*Publishers*
1 London Bridge Street
London SE1 9GF

www.harpercollins.co.uk

The Secret of Happy Children first published in Australia in 1984
as a Bay Books Publication, revised 1988, 1993, 1995, 1998.
More Secrets of Happy Children first published in Australia in 1994
as a Bay Books Publication, revised 1995, 1998.
The Complete Secrets of Happy Children first published in 2002
by Cornstalk, an imprint of HarperCollins*Publishers*.
This edition published 2015 by Thorsons

19

A catalogue record of this book is
available from the British Library

ISBN 978-0-00-716174-4

Printed and bound in China by
RR Donnelley APS

MIX
Paper from
responsible sources
FSC™ C007454

FSC is a non-profit international organisation established to promote the responsible management of the world's forests. Products carrying the FSC label are independently certified to assure consumers that they come from forests that are managed to meet the social, economic and ecological needs of present and future generations.

Find out more about HarperCollins and the environment at
www.harpercollins.co.uk/green

About the Author

Steve Biddulph started as a family psychologist twenty years ago. Realizing he didn't have a clue, he travelled and learned from some of the best practitioners in Australia, the US, New Zealand and Singapore during the early days of family therapy. Throughout this time he worked with hundreds of families in both normal and extreme situations, and saw the need for positive and helpful books for parents.

The worldwide success of *The Secret of Happy Children* has led him to work mostly in parent education. Steve gives talks about discipline without hitting or shaming, raising boys to be safe men, and other topics, in countries as diverse as China, Germany, England and South Africa. His books are published in fifteen languages. He has also specialized in helping people recover from childhood trauma, abuse and neglect, and trains professionals in these skills.

Steve and his partner Shaaron live on the NSW north coast, where they write books and try their best to live out their ideals.

Thanks to all in the Transactional Analysis community from the early seventies onwards, especially Colin McKenzie, Pat McKenzie, the Maslens, the Mellors, and Jean Grigor. These people both saved my life, and set me on this wonderful road. To my parents for a good start. To my partner Shaaron Biddulph for all that she has taught and given me. To Doro, June and everyone at Parent Network for bringing my work to England. To everyone at Thorsons UK. And to all of us parents everywhere, for struggling on and still remembering how to laugh.

Contents

The Secrets of Happy Children

More Secrets of Happy Children

The story behind this book

When I first wrote *The Secret of Happy Children*, I never dreamed that it would take off in quite the way it has. Ten years after first cranking up the typewriter, it has been read by over a million people, in thirteen languages. I now spend a fair portion of my time giving talks to audiences around the world who have been attracted either by the book, or its reputation, or else the fact that there's nothing good on television that night!

I wrote *The Secret* when I was still a beginning Family Therapist, with a heartfelt wish to make it easier for fathers and mothers to get along well with their kids, and for kids to live without the put-downs and fears that our generation often felt.

The first edition announced on the first page that I had no children, only wombats (and that these were quite badly behaved!). I mentioned this because it was true, and because I wanted my readers to take everything I said with a pinch of salt – to trust their own judgement. I still believe this – experts are a hazard to your health! Your own heart will always tell you, if you listen to it, what is the best way to raise your children. Books, experts, friends, courses, help you only if they take you closer to your own heart.

I do have kids now and wombats. I still feel an aching in my chest everytime I see a young mum with a new baby, or a young dad taking his kids to the shops, and trying, as we all try, to get it right and give these kids the best start we possibly can.

I'm proud to be launching this new edition. Thousands of parents have told me, to my face, that they found the ideas in this book powerful and helpful. Much that they have taught me has been incorporated to make the book even better.

We all need love and encouragement to do the job – to raise happy, healthy, loving kids.

Here's my love and encouragement to you.

Steve Biddulph

Foreword

Why are so many adults unhappy?

Think of all the people who have problems – who lack confidence, cannot make a decision, worry about little details, can't relax, or can't make friends with other people. Think of those who are aggressive, putting people down and ignoring the needs of those around them. Add to the above all those just holding on until the next drink or the next tranquilliser.

In one of the richest, most peaceful countries in the world, unhappiness is epidemic. One adult in every five will at some time need psychiatric care, one marriage in three ends in divorce, one adult in four needs medication to relax. It's a great life!

Unemployment and difficult economic circumstances don't help, but unhappiness is present in all income groups – rich, poor and in-between. It's a problem, in fact, that no amount of money seems to solve.

On the other hand, we are often puzzled by some people's constant cheerfulness and optimism. Why is it that, in some individuals, the human spirit blossoms in spite of apparent hardship?

The fact of the matter is that many people have unhappiness programmed into them. They have been unwittingly taught to be unhappy and are simply living out the script. When reading this book you may realise that, by accident, you are hypnotising your children into disliking themselves, and causing them to have problems which may last a lifetime.

How this happens and how to change it – in fact, how to create happy children – is what this book is all about.

The Secrets of Happy Children

1

Seeds in the mind

You hypnotise your children every single day. You may as well do it properly!

It's nine o'clock at night and I'm sitting in my office with a tearful fifteen-year old girl. She is dressed in fashionable, older-than-her-years clothes, but the effect is only to make her look more helpless and child-like. We are talking about the fact that she is pregnant and what can be done about it.

This is familiar ground for me, and for anyone who works with teenagers. It doesn't mean, though, that it can be hurried. What matters is that, for the young woman sitting in front of me, this is the worst day of her life and she needs all the support, time and clarity, that I can offer. About all, she must make her own decision.

I ask about her parents' likely reaction – when they find out. She almost spits out the answer.

'Oh, they'll say they told me so. They always said I'd never amount to nothing!'

Later, as I drive home, that one sentence stays in my mind. 'They always said I'd never amount to nothing.' I've often heard parents talk to kids like that.

'You're hopeless.'
'God, you're a nuisance.'
'You'll be sorry, just you see.'
'You're as bad as your Uncle Merv' (who's in jail).
'You're just like your Auntie Eve' (who's fond of a drink).
'You're crazy, do you hear?'

This is the kind of programming that many youngsters grow up with; it is passed on unwittingly by overwrought parents and continues as a kind of family curse down the generations. It's called a *self-fulfilling prophecy* because saying it often enough makes it come true. Children, with their brilliant, perceptive, strangely co-operative ways, will usually live up to our expectations!

These are extreme examples, which we'd all recognise at once as destructive. Most negative programming, however, is much more subtle. Observe children playing in a vacant block, climbing trees. 'You'll fall! Watch out! You'll slip!' cries the voice of the anxious mother from over the fence.

The slightly drunk father ends a half-hearted argument with his wife, who goes off in a 'huff' to buy some cigarettes. 'There y'are son, never trust a woman. They'll just use y'up.' The seven-year-old looks up solemnly and nods. Yes, Dad.

And in a million sitting rooms and kitchens:

'God, you're lazy.'
'You're so selfish.'
'You silly idiot, stop that.'
'Dumb!'
'Give it to me, stupid!'
'Don't be such a pest.'

What we have discovered is that this kind of comment doesn't only have the obvious effect of making the child feel bad momentarily. Put-downs also have a *hypnotic effect* and act unconsciously, like seeds in the mind, seeds which will grow and shape the person's self-image, eventually becoming true facts about the child's personality.

How do we hypnotise our children?

Hypnosis and suggestion have long been a source of fascination to people. They seem slightly mystical and unreal and yet are well accepted scientifically. Most people have witnessed them, perhaps as part of a stage show, for getting help to cure a habit, or for relaxation.

We are familiar with the key elements of hypnosis: the use of some device to distract the mind ('vatch ze vatch'), the commanding tone ('you will feel nothing'), and the rhythmic, repetitious tone of the hypnotist's speech. We also know about post-hypnotic suggestion, the ability to implant a command which the unsuspecting person later carries out, often to his or her dismay, at a given signal. It all makes for good theatre, but also for excellent therapy in the hands of a qualified practitioner.

What most people don't realise, however, is that *hypnosis is an everyday event.* Whenever we use certain patterns of speech, we reach into the unconscious minds of our children and program them, even though we have no such intention.

The old concept – that hypnosis required an altered state of mind, or trance – has been abandoned. This was only one form of unconscious learning. The rather frightening truth is that the human mind can be programmed in normal waking life beneath the awareness of the person involved. Already in the US, many sales and advertising people are being trained in the use of hypnotic methods embedded in normal business conversation – a chilling concept (*For more details, see 'Further Information' in the Appendix.*) Fortunately hypnosis requires great skill to use in a manipulative way, and can be countered if the subject becomes aware of the process. Accidental hypnosis, though, is so much part of everyday life that parents – without realising it – implant messages in their child's mind, and these messages, unless strongly contradicted, will echo on for a lifetime.

Hypnotised without knowing it

The late Dr Milton Erikson was recognised as the world's foremost hypnotist. He was once called upon to treat a man who suffered extreme pain from cancer, was refusing to have hypnosis and was not being helped by painkillers. Erikson simply stopped by his private ward and talked about the man's hobby of growing tomatoes.

A careful listener could have detected the unusual rhythm in Erikson's speech and the stressing of odd phrases, like 'deep down' (in-the soil), growing 'good and strong', 'easy' (to pick), 'warm and loose' (in the glasshouse). Also, the observer could have noted that Erikson's face and posture changed very slightly as he spoke those key phrases. The man in question simply thought that it was a pleasant exchange. Until he died, however, five days later, as doctors knew he must, the man felt no pain.

'You' messages

A child's mind is full of questions. Perhaps the greatest of these are the questions, 'Who am I?', 'What kind of person am I?', 'Where do I fit in?'. These are the questions of self-definition, or identity, upon which we base our lives as adults, and from which we make all our key decisions. Because of this a child's mind is remarkably affected by statements which begin with the words, 'You are'.

Whether the message is 'You are so lazy' or 'You're a great kid', these statements from the important 'big' people will go deeply and firmly into the child's unconsciousness. I have heard so many adults, overcome by a life crisis, recalling what they were told as a child: 'I'm so useless, I know I am'.

Psychologists, like many professional groups, tend to complicate things just a little, and call these statements 'attributions'. These attributions crop up again and again in adult life.

Johnny!
You'll slip on a foothold and miss your grip and fall and fracture your pelvis, and cut your carotid artery on that glass and the ambulance will go to the wrong suburb, and you'll lose two pints of blood and be in intensive care for months and then how do you think I'll feel?

'Why don't you apply for that promotion?'
'No, I'm not good enough.'

'But he's just like your last husband. Why did you marry him?'
'I'm just stupid, I guess.'

'Why do you let them push you around like that?'
'That's the story of my life.'

These words – 'not good enough', 'just stupid', did not come out of the blue. They are recorded in people's brains because they were said to them at an age when they were unable to question their truthfulness. 'But surely,' I can hear you saying, 'children must disagree with the "you" messages they are given?'

Certainly children think about the things that are said to them, checking for accuracy. But they may have no comparisons. At times we are all lazy, selfish, untidy, stupid, forgetful, mischievous, and so on. The preacher in the old-time church was on a sure thing when he thundered out, 'You have sinned!' – everyone had!

'Adults know everything; they can even read your mind.' Such are the thoughts of a child. So when a child is told 'You're clumsy', he or she becomes nervous, and *is* clumsy. The child told 'You're a pest' feels the rejection, becomes desperate for reassurance and so *does* pester. The child told 'You're an idiot' may violently disagree on the outside, but inside can only sadly agree. You're the adult, so you must be right.

'You' messages work at *both* the conscious and unconscious levels. In our work we've often asked children to describe themselves, and they will say things like 'I'm a bad kid', 'I'm a nuisance'.

Others, though, will show evidence of confusion – 'Mum and Dad say they love me, but I don't think they do'. Consciously they hear the words, but unconsciously they hear/see/smell the feeling behind the words.

It's all in the way we say it. We can choose to say to children, 'I'm angry with you and I want you to tidy up your toys NOW!' and have

YOU ARE BEAUTIFUL!
I Am not!

no fears about lasting effects. If we say, 'You lazy little brat, why don't you ever do what you're told?' and repeat this kind of message whenever conflict occurs, then the result will come as no surprise.

Don't pretend to be happy or loving when you aren't feeling that way – it's confusing and can make children become evasive and in time quite disturbed. We can be honest about our feelings, without putting children down. They can handle 'I'm really tired today', or 'Right now I'm too angry…' especially if this matches what they have sensed all along. It helps them realise that you are human too, which has got to be a good thing.

At a large parents' meeting I once addressed, I asked if people would call out the 'you' messages they remembered hearing as children. I wrote them on a blackboard and this is what we came up with:

You're lazy clumsy stupid
a nuisance just a girl
too young to understand
selfish dumb
a pest dirty
thoughtless inconsiderate
always late greedy
bad-tempered brainless noisy
gutless a worry crazy
mental making your mother sick
ugly plain immature
just like your father
…and on it went.

The examples came in little rushes at first, as people's memories were triggered, but by the end the blackboard was covered and the room was almost in a state of riot. The sense of relief and release was very evident in the large hall as people spoke aloud the words that had hurt them so long ago.

Very few people felt their parents had been deliberately destructive or malicious – it was simply that this was the way children were corrected. 'Tell them they're bad and that makes them good!' Those were the Dark Ages of child-rearing: we're just beginning to escape.

Your mind remembers everything that ever happened to you

In the 1950s people with epilepsy had a bad time because the medications we now use had not been developed. A man called Penfield found that an operation could be used to help the more severe cases. By making small cuts on the surface of a person's brain, he could sometimes reduce or even halt the 'electrical storms' which cause epileptic seizures.

The interesting part – I hope you're sitting down as you read this – is that the patients were required, for safety reasons, to be conscious, and the operation was done under only a local anaesthetic. The surgeon removed a small piece of skull, made the cuts and then put back the piece and sewed up the skin. It makes me shudder, too, but it was better than the disease!

During the operation the patients experienced something very surprising. As the doctor, using a fine probe, made tiny contacts with the surface of the brain, the patient would suddenly have vivid recollections – watching *Gone with the Wind* years earlier, complete with the smell of cheap perfume in the cinema and the beehive hairstyle of the person in front! When the doctor moved the probe to another spot, the person would see before him his fourth birthday party – even though he was wide awake and sitting in the operating chair. It was the same with every patient, though of course the memories were different.

Subsequent research backed up this remarkable discovery: that everything – every sight, sound and spoken word – is stored in our brain. It is often difficult to remember but nevertheless it is there, having its effect. On the wrinkled surface of our brain our life is recorded in its entirety!

Unconscious hearing is a phenomenon that you've almost certainly experienced. You've been at a party or a meeting, listening to someone near you. The room is buzzing with people talking and perhaps music, too. Suddenly, from a conversation clear across the room, you hear someone say your name, or the name of a friend, or something that concerns you. 'Aaargh!' you think, 'what are they saying about me?'

How does this happen? We have discovered from research that there are two parts to your hearing: firstly, what your ears actually pick up; and secondly, what you pay conscious attention to.

Although you are unaware of it, your brilliant hearing system is filtering every conversation within range in the room and, if a key word or phrase occurs, the switchboard department in your brain 'puts it through' to conscious attention. You certainly couldn't listen to all that was being said at one time but, nonetheless, a primitive filter is scanning it for important messages. We know this from many experiments and also from the fact that under hypnosis people can recall things that they didn't consciously notice at the time!

The following situation has been reported in many parts of the world.

Late one night a petrol tanker runs out of control, careers downhill and smashes through the front wall of a house. When rescuers enter the house they are amazed to find a young mother sleeping heavily, undisturbed by the crash. As they stand there, not knowing what to do, a baby begins to cry in the back room. The mother instantly awakes. 'Wha...what's going on?'

The filter in her hearing system works on as she sleeps but is checking for only one thing – the baby – and only this sound is 'put through' to her mind.

How does all of the above relate to children? Think of all the things that are said about children when they are supposedly not listening. Then remember their acute listening powers (a sweet wrapper at 50 metres!). We may well include the time when they are asleep for there is clear evidence that sounds and speech are taken in even as a person dreams and sleeps.

Also, there is that obvious time when a child has not yet learnt (or decided to let you know) that it can speak. The baby, for months before it speaks much, can follow much of what is intended, if not every word.

I am often amazed by parents, who have been fighting bitterly for years or are desperately unhappy for some reason, telling me, 'Of course, the kids know nothing about it'. Children, in fact, know almost everything about everything. They may oblige you by keeping it to themselves or only show it indirectly by bedwetting or trying to murder their siblings, but they know. So, if you talk about your children, be sure you are saying what you really want to say. This, too, is a direct channel to their minds.

And why not start to use this channel to boost them by saying what you genuinely like and appreciate to others while they're in earshot? This is especially useful at ages/stages when direct praise is embarrassing to them.

Hearing and healing

This story is told by one of my teachers, Dr Virginia Satir.

A child had just been operated on for tonsil removal and, back in the ward, was failing to stop bleeding. Dr Satir joined the concerned staff in examining the still-open cuts in the child's throat.

On an impulse, she asked what was happening in the theatre at the time of the operation.

'Oh, we'd just finished a throat cancer operation on an old lady.'

'What were you talking about.'

'Oh that last operation, and how she didn't have much chance of living – there was too much damage.'

Dr Satir's mind worked fast. She saw the child undergoing the simple and routine procedure, under general anaesthetic, while the staff talked about the previous patient: 'not much chance of living', 'pretty bad shape'.

Quickly, she asked that the child be taken back to the theatre. She instructed the staff in what to say:

'Gee this kid looks good and healthy, not like the old lady we operated on before.' 'This kid has a nice healthy throat.' 'She'll be healed in a jiffy and back playing with her friends!'

The bleeding stopped, the anaesthetic wore off and the child went home the next day.

Anchoring Anchoring is one of the most recent discoveries in hypnosis. Scientists have realised that a message goes most deeply into a person's mind if it is accompanied by other signals that reinforce it.

This is really quite simple.

If a person says to you, 'You're a pest!', you will probably feel rather put out. If he says it with a frown and a loud voice, this will be worse. If he says it very loudly, moves towards you whilst making menacing movements and appears somewhat out of control, then you have a problem.

If he happens to be three times larger than you and is one of your family – on whom your well-being depends – you will probably remember the incident for the rest of your life.

Modern-day men and women, especially those of us of Anglo-Saxon descent, tend to be constrained in our day-to-day life. We do not act or speak with very much passion or force. It's not that we are low-key and relaxed – just more controlled and bottled up. We tend to keep our good and bad feelings to ourselves and, when things go badly, we try to carry the burden without giving any outward signs. Consequently, when we finally do blow up or break down, we often surprise both ourselves and those around us. If the feeling being released is anger and frustration, then those around us may feel that we have lost control and are dangerous to them...and we may agree!

Because of this, our children may live in a situation where day-to-day messages are fairly vague and indirect: 'Now don't do that, darling, come along', 'There's a good boy'. Both positive and negative messages are casual and not great in their impact.

Then, one day, when life has really overloaded Mum or Dad, there comes a powerful outburst, 'You little brat, I wish you'd shut up', anchored with wild eyes, sudden, close proximity, never-before-heard volume and a sense of quivering lack of control that is quite unforgettable. The message is inescapable, although untrue: this is what Mum or Dad really thinks of me!

The words that overwrought parents choose at these times can be remarkably strong.

'I wish you'd never been born.'
'You're a stupid, stupid child.'
'You're killing me, do you hear?'
'I'd like to throttle you!'

It's not bad to get angry at or around children. On the contrary, children need to learn that one can be angry and discharge tension and be heard, in safety. Elizabeth Kubler Ross says that real anger lasts 20 seconds and is mostly noise. The problem comes when the positive messages ('You are great', 'We love you', 'We'll look after you') are not equally strong or reliable. Often, although we feel these, we do not communicate them.

Almost every child is dearly loved, but many children do not know this fact; many adults will go to their death still believing that they were a nuisance and a disappointment to their parents. It is one of the most moving moments in family therapy to be able to clear away this misunderstanding.

At the times when a child's life goes shaky – when a new baby is brought home, when a marriage breaks up, when failure occurs at school, when there is no work for a hopeful teenager – it is important to give positive messages, anchored with a hand on a shoulder and a clear look in the eye: whatever happens, you are special and important to us. We know you're great.

So far we've talked about the *unconscious* programming of children to be unhappy adults. There are lots of direct ways too!

WHAT NOT TO DO

When disciplining, use put-downs instead of simple demands.

Use put-downs in a friendly way; say, as a pet-name.

Compare!

Set an example!

Talk to other people about children's faults in their hearing.

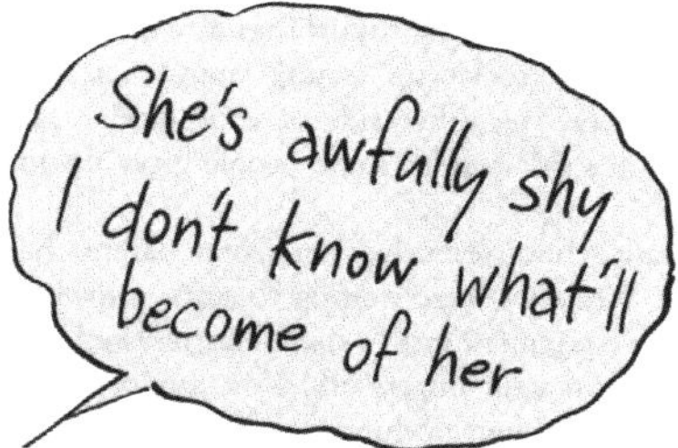

Take pride in patterns that are bound to cause trouble later.

Use guilt to control children.

These sorts of statements can be left out of your parenting repertoire for good. You and they will feel better for it.

I'LL GIVE YOU CRAZY!

Have you ever listened to yourself talking to your kids, and just moaned? A lot of the things we say to kids are, well, crazy! Scots comedian Billy Connolly bemoaned some of these in a recent concert we heard...(you'll have to imagine the accent).

'Mum, can I go to the pictures?' 'Pictures! I'll give you pictures.'

'Can I have some bread then?' 'Bread! I'll bread you my boy!'

Most of us can remember being told things as a child which simply made no sense at all, phrases like: pull your socks up young man...if you don't come to your senses soon...you'll smile on the other side of your face!...I'll teach you to make a fool of me!...and so on. It's no wonder some people grow up to be a little confused.

I was in a primary school recently where some parents had brought their toddlers to join a new play group. While we were waiting to start, a lively and curious little boy started to pull out some maths equipment from a shelf. His harassed-looking mum told him 'If you touch that the teacher will cut your fingers off!' Now any of us can understand the motivation to say this kind of thing – when nothing else works, try terror! But with this kind of message coming thick and fast, what can a child conclude about life? It can only go two ways: either the world is a crazy and dangerous place, or else, it's no good listening to Mum, she talks a load of rubbish. Now there's the start of a well adjusted life. We've all done it!

One day (true confession) I told my two-year-old son that the police might be cross with him if he didn't wear his seatbelt. I was hot and tired, and I hate squirming my six-foot-four frame around inside cars to fasten seatbelt buckles on protesting kids. I resorted to a cheap trick, and I paid the price. As soon as the words came out of my mouth I regretted it. For days after I had questions thick and fast. 'Do the policemen have guns?', 'Are there any policemen down this road?' It was a major job of rehabilitation to get him back to feeling calm, and comfortable about the men and women in blue.

We shouldn't have to explain everything to our kids, or endlessly reason with them till we are blue in the face. 'Because I say so' is a good enough reason some of the time. But there is nothing ever to be gained by needlessly scaring them. 'When your father gets home...' 'You'll make me so sick I'll have to go away...' 'We'll put you into a home...' are the kinds of messages that harm and haunt even tough children. We are their main source of information early on, and later our credibility is put to the test (since they have or will have other sources to compare us with). Our job is to give them a realistic, even slightly rosy picture of the world – which they can build on as they go, and so become hardy and secure on the inside. When they encounter trickiness or dishonesty later in life, they will at least know that this isn't completely the way of the world, that some people are trustworthy, and safe to be around – Mum and Dad included.

Why do parents put children down?

At this point, you could be feeling guilty about the way that you speak to your own children. Please don't get these ideas out of perspective. There is a lot that can be done to overcome old programming whether your children are still little or even if they are now adults.

The first step is to begin understanding yourself, to know why put-downs became part of your parenting in the first place. Almost every parent is guilty of unnecessary put-downs from time to time. There are three main reasons for this.

1. You say what was said to you!

You weren't taught about parenting in school: you had to start from scratch when your children were born and work it out for yourself. But you did have one clear example to work from – your own parents.

I'm sure you've found yourself in a heated moment yelling out and then thinking, 'Good grief, that's what my parents used to say to me and I hated it!' Those old tape recordings are your 'automatic pilot', however, and it takes presence of mind and practice to react in ways you really prefer.

Some parents, of course, go to the other extreme. With painful memories of the way in which they were raised, they swear never to scold, hit or deprive their own children. The danger here is that they may overdo it, and their children suffer from a lack of control. It isn't easy, is it?

2. You just thought it was the right thing to do!

It was once thought that kids were basically bad, and the thing to do was to tell them how bad they were. This would shame them into being better!

Perhaps you were brought up in this way. As a parent you simply hadn't thought about self-esteem or the need to help children gain confidence. If so, I hope that what you are reading has changed your mind. Now that you realise how put-downs damage children, I'm sure you'll be keen to stop using them.

When money is short, or you are overworked, lonely or bored, or because being at home isn't enough for you, then you are much more likely to be destructive in what you say to kids.

3. You are down on your own reserves

The reasons for this are clear. When we are pressured in any way we build up a body tension which needs discharging. It actually does feel good to lash out at someone, in words or actions.

Children suffer because they are easier to get angry with than your spouse, boss, landlord, or whomever. It's important to think it through: I feel so tense! Who am I *really* angry with?

The relief of lashing out is short-lived since the child is likely to behave even more badly as a result but at the time it feels like a release.

If this happens, it is vitally important that you find a safe way to let off steam.

Tension can be dissipated in two ways:

1) by vigorous action, such as hitting a mattress, doing some vigorous work, going for a brisk walk. This is no small matter – many a child's life has been saved by being shut in its bedroom while a distraught parent walks for miles as a means of calming down;
2) by dissolving the tension through talking with a friend, finding affection from a partner (if you're fortunate enough to have one) or through some activity such as yoga, sport or massage that releases tension out of your body.

Eventually, as a parent, you must learn to care for yourself as much as for your children. You actually do more for your kids by spending some time each day on your own (your health, your relaxation) than by being totally devoted to serving them.

So, that's the end of the bad news. The rest of this book is about how to do it the easier way! It is possible to change, and many parents have told me that just hearing about these ideas at a meeting or on the radio has helped them immediately.

Already while you've been reading, your ideas have been changing. You'll find that, without even trying, your behaviour with your children will start to be easier and more positive. I promise!

Craigette
Come Here
Now
GEEZ
IT
WORKED!
ZOOOOOM

THE WAY YOU SAY IT – POSITIVE WORDING MAKES COMPETENT KIDS

It's not only praise or put-downs that determine a child's level of confidence. There are some other important ways we program our kids – particularly by the way we give instructions and commands – in a negative or positive choice of words.

As adults, we guide our own behaviour and feelings by 'self-talk', the chatter that goes on inside our heads. ('Better not forget to get petrol', 'Oh geez I forgot my purse, I must be getting senile' etc.) Psychologists are amazed at the differences between how healthy, happy people, and unwell or distressed people, talk to themselves mentally. Self-talk is learned directly from your parents or teachers. With your own kids then, it's a great chance to put in all sorts of positive and useful data, which your child can internalise – a comfortable and encouraging part of themselves for life.

Children learn how to guide and organise themselves internally, from the way we guide and organise them with our words, so it pays to be positive. For example, we can say to a child, 'For goodness sake don't get into any fights at school today!' or we can say 'I want you to have a good time at school and only play with the kids you like'.

Why should such a small thing make a difference? It's all in the way the human mind works. If someone offered you a million dollars not to think of a blue monkey for two minutes – you wouldn't be able to do it (try it now if you don't believe us!). If a child is told 'Don't fall out of the tree', then they have to think two things: 'Don't' and 'fall out of the tree'. Because we used those words, they automatically create this picture. What we think, we automatically rehearse. (Imagine biting hard into a lemon, and notice how you react just to the fantasy!) A child who is vividly imagining falling out of a tree is much more likely to do so. Far better to use positive wording: 'Hold on to the tree carefully', 'Keep your mind on what you're doing'.

There are dozens of chances each day to get this right. Rather than say '*Don't* run out into the traffic', it's easier and better to say '*Stay* on the footpath close to me' – so that the child imagines what to do, and not what not to do.

Give kids clear instructions as to the right way to do things. Kids don't always know how to be safe, so make your commands specific: 'Tracey, hold on firmly to the side of the boat with both your hands' is much more powerful than 'Don't you dare fall out' or worse still 'How do you think I'll feel if you drown?' The changes are small but the difference is obvious.

Of course, learning to talk like this doesn't occur by waving a magic wand. You will still need to back yourself up with action. By using positive wording, you will be helping your kids to think and act positively, and to feel capable in a wide range of situations, because they know what to do, and aren't scaring themselves about what not to do.

SPECIAL DISCOVERY – NEW VITAMINS CHILDREN NEED

We all know about the vitamins A to K, which we need in our daily diet to thrive and grow. It is rumoured that scientists have recently discovered some more vitamins which are just as essential. Here they are:

VITAMIN M – for music. Naturally occurring in young parents, can be added to family's diet immediately. Put on great music and dance with the kids in your living room – often. Pick them up if they are too small, and dance around with them. Sing in the car, collect favourite tapes. Have some simple instruments around. If you take your kids to music lessons, make sure they are satisfying, or at least good fun, for your child.

VITAMIN P – for poetry. Teach little chants and rhymes to toddlers. Older kids can recite and perform favourite short poems at family gatherings. Listen to stories and poetry on tape to enjoy the spoken voice.

VITAMIN N – for nature. Make chances for your children to experience total non-human environments. For little kids, a back yard will do – lots of wild insects and crawlies, bird-attracting shrubs and trees. But whenever you can, get into the bush, and go to the beach. Watch sunsets. Camp out. Closely related to Vitamin S for spirituality, sometimes available at churches, temples, mosques and similar.

VITAMIN F – for fun. Available anywhere. Rubs off from children onto adults, and back again. Most common vitamin in the universe. Not naturally present in the workplace, but can be smuggled in.

VITAMIN H – for hope. Hope is naturally occurring. You just have to make sure it isn't removed by exposure to toxins. Avoid watching the news or viewing the world through newspapers. Don't indulge in gloom-mongering around kids – especially teenagers. Join something that makes a difference – Greenpeace, Friends of the Earth, WWW – whose publications are incredibly positive. Research has shown that kids with even slightly activist parents are more mentally healthy, have a more positive view of the world and the future, and do more about it.

2

What children really want

It's cheaper than video games, and healthier than ice-cream!

The question that is uppermost in the minds of millions of parents can be summed up in one word...

Why do kids play up? Why do they always explore where they shouldn't, do things that are not allowed, fight, tease, disobey, provoke, argue, make a mess, and generally seem to want to persecute Mum and Dad?

Why do some kids actually seem to enjoy getting into trouble?

This chapter tells you what is going on inside 'naughty' children, and how 'bad' behaviour is actually the result of good (healthy) forces going astray.

After reading this chapter, you'll be able not only to see sense in children's misbehaviour but you'll also be able to act to prevent and convert it, making yourself and your children much happier.

You don't believe me, do you? Read on!

Children play up for one reason only: they have *unmet needs*. 'But what needs,' you are thinking, 'do my children have that are unmet? I feed them, clothe them, buy them toys, keep them warm and clean...'

Well, there are some extra needs (luckily very cheap to provide) which go beyond the 'basics' mentioned. These mysterious needs are essential, not only to make happy children but to maintain life itself. Perhaps I can explain best by telling a story.

In 1945, the Second World War ended and Europe lay in ruins. Among the many human problems to be tackled was that of caring for the thousands of orphans whose parents had either been killed or permanently separated from them by the war.

The Swiss, who had managed to stay out of the war itself, sent their health workers out to begin tackling some of these problems; one man, a doctor, was given the job of researching how to best care for the orphan babies.

He travelled about Europe and visited many kinds of orphan-care situations, to see what was the most successful type of care. He saw many extremes. In some places, American field hospitals had been set up and the babies were snug in stainless steel cots, in hygienic wards, getting their four-hourly feeds of special milk formula from crisply uniformed nurses.

At the other end of the scale, in remote mountain villages, a truck had simply pulled up, the driver had asked, 'Can you look after these babies?' and left half-a-dozen crying infants in the care of the villagers. Here, surrounded by kids, dogs, goats, in the arms of the village women, the babies took their chances on goat's milk and the communal stewpot.

The Swiss doctor had a simple way of comparing the different forms of care. No need even to weigh the babies, far less measure co-ordination or look for smiling and eye contact. In those days of influenza and dysentery, he used the simplest of all statistics – the death rate.

And what he discovered was rather a surprise…as epidemics raged through Europe and many people were dying, the children in the rough villages were thriving better than their scientifically-cared-for counterparts in the hospitals!

The doctor had discovered something that old wives had known for a long time but no one had really listened. He had discovered that babies need *love* to live.

The infants in the field hospital had everything but affection and stimulation. The babies in the villages had more hugs, bounces and things to see than they knew what to do with and, given reasonable basic care, were thriving.

Of course, the doctor didn't use the word '*love*' (words like that upset scientists) but he spelt it out clearly enough. What was important, he said, was:

- skin-to-skin contact frequently, and from two or three special people;
- movement of a gentle but robust kind, such as carrying around, bouncing on a knee, and so on

- eye contact, smiling, and a colourful, lively environment; sounds such as singing, talking, goo-gooing, and so on.

It was an important discovery, and the first time that it had been stated in writing. Babies need human contact and affection (and not just to be fed, warmed and cleaned). If they are not given this, they may easily die.

So much for babies. But what about older children?

Here is an interesting thing – on page 32 is a graph of my estimate of the amount of touching (that's right, physical touching) that people receive as their lives unfold.

Remember, this is the average situation. Who knows what is the ideal – perhaps a line straight across. You may be wondering about the dip at about two to three years of age. That's when child number two (or three or four) usually comes along and affection has to be shared – a rough time for everyone!

Little babies like to be touched and cuddled. So do small children, although they are choosier about who does the cuddling. Teenagers often get awkward about it, but will admit in trust that they like affection as much as anyone. And, of course, by late teens they are pursuing specialised forms of affection with great energy!

I once asked an audience of about 60 adults to close their eyes and raise their hands if they got less affection than they would like to get in

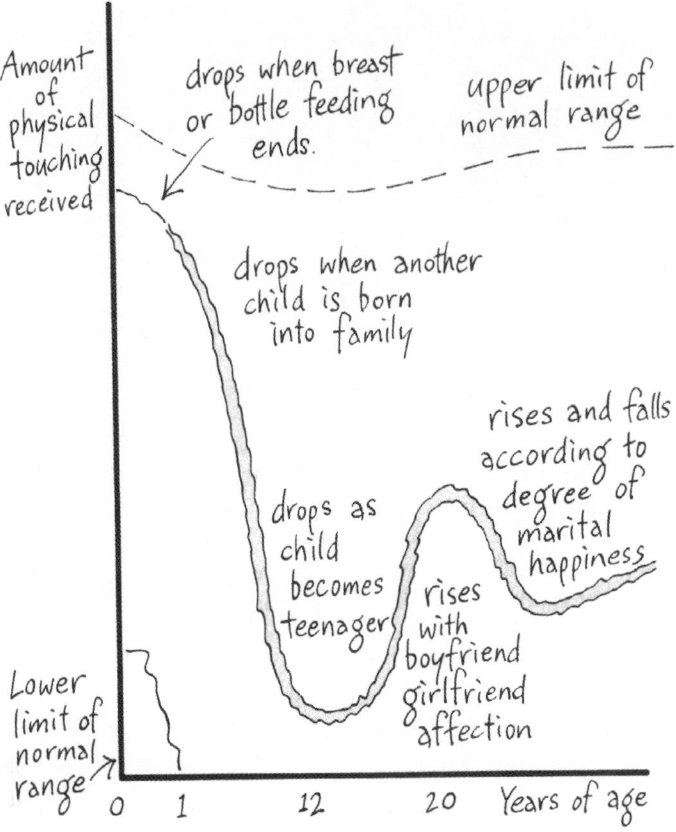

daily life. It was unanimous – every hand went up. After a minute the peeping began and the room began to ring with laughter. From this careful scientific study, I conclude that adults need affection, too.

Apart from physical touch, we find other ways to get good feelings from people. The most obvious one is by using words.

We need to be recognised, noticed and, preferably, given sincere praise. We want to be included in conversations, have our ideas listened to and even admired.

A three-year-old says it out straight: 'Hey, look at me.'

Many rich people take little pleasure in their bank balance unless it can be displayed and someone is there to notice.

I am sometimes reduced to stitches by the realisation that most of the adult world is made up of three-year-olds running about shouting, 'Look at me, Daddy', 'Watch me, you guys'. Not me, of course – I give lectures and write books out of mature adult concern.

So, an interesting picture emerges. We take care of our children's bodily needs but, if this is all we do, they still miss out. They have psychological needs, too, and these are simple but essential. A child needs stimulation, of a human kind. He must have a diet of talking each day, with some affection and praise added in, in order to be happy. If this is given fully, and not begrudgingly from behind a pile of ironing or a newspaper, then it will not even take very long!

Many people reading this will already have older children, or teenagers. You may be thinking, 'But already they have learned some bad ways of getting attention. How can I deal with that?'

Here is another story.

'Of mice and men'

A few years ago, psychologists went about in white coats and worked mostly with rats. (Nowadays they wear sports coats and work mostly with housewives – things are looking up!) The 'rat psychologists' were able to learn a lot about behaviour because they could do things with rats that they couldn't do with children. Read on, and you'll see what I mean.

In this particular experiment, rats were placed in a special cage, with food and drink, and a little lever. They ate, drank and ran about, and eventually asked themselves the same question you are asking: 'What's the lever for?' They pressed it (being like children, they wanted to try everything) and, to their surprise, a little window opened in the cage to reveal a film being shown on the wall outside. The window soon closed and the rat had to press the lever again to get more of the movie.

of course he only does it for the attention

TALKING IS BRAIN-FOOD FOR KIDS...

By the time they reach school age, some kids can talk very well and have a wide vocabulary. Some on the other hand are very limited in their verbal skills. This can be a real disadvantage – for one thing, teachers often use talking skills as an indicator of intelligence and ability, and so your kids can be either deliberately, or unconsciously, labelled as 'slow'. How can you help your kids to be good with words – not little Einsteins, but able to speak up for themselves? Here's how...

It was found as early as the 1950s that parents fall into two distinct groups in their approaches to talking to children. Some parents are very abrupt and short in what they say to their kids:

'Dwayne, shut that bleedin' door!', 'Get here', 'Eat it!' and so on. Others were the opposite: 'Charles sweetheart, would you mind closing the door – it's blowing quite a draught on little Sebastian, there's a good boy!'

You don't have to be a professor to see that young Charles is going to have more words in his little head than Dwayne, and more ways of stringing them together. (Though on the other hand Dwayne may also know some that Charles doesn't!)

A lot of parents now are more aware of talking to their children, explaining things and just chatting to them for the pleasure of it. They have realised the first rule of children and language – they always understand more than they show.

Here are the basic steps...

1) During pregnancy make lots of sounds to and around your baby. You can start by singing or crooning when you feel like it, having music playing (quite loudly is fine). If you're a Dad, snuggle up and talk to your wife or even directly to the baby! This way your child will come to know and feel safe with your manly voice and be easier for you to comfort when they are little. Repetition and familiarity helps – the sound of TV's *Days of Our Lives* theme music has been found to soothe new-borns who 'listened' to it with Mum during pregnancy!
2) With infants continue all this talk, singing, and music exposure once the baby is born. Moving or swinging them about will add to their delight and sense of rhythm, which is a necessary part of speech. (Special movies have been used to show that we all do a subtle swaying dance as we speak – that it is almost impossible to be still while speaking.) If you can carry the baby about with you in a sling or harness as you work, all the better.

As you go through the day with toddlers, tell them about what you are doing, using simple words, but not all baby talk. Use repetition of those words they say to you, so as to polish up what they are saying.

3) As toddlers start to talk more you can help by echoing and adding to what they say to you, so they are both encouraged by the response, and helped to get the words right.

'Buppa!'. 'You want the butter?', 'Want buppa!'

and a little later

'Pass butta ayy?', 'You want me to pass the butter?', 'Pass me butter?' and so on!

The best way to do all this is casually – as a game – with no undue pressure or expectations.

A recent TV series featured interviews with 'superbright' or 'hothouse' kids. It gave us some mixed feelings – these kids were certainly high achievers, but some by adulthood had turned into real oddballs! One family though stood out – for the naturalness and balance of their kids. All four daughters ranging from eight to sixteen in age were friendly, relaxed, very down-to-earth, and yet extraordinarily advanced in their skills. The sixteen-year-old for instance had simply skipped primary school (at her teacher's suggestion – the parents had been quite happy for her to go) – She was now doing doctoral research into spinal cell damage. Asked how they had raised such genius kids, the father said 'It couldn't be genetic – I haven't had the sperm bank knocking on my door!' (And he did look, well, rather ordinary!) The mother added that 'We just explain things to them…' She explained that as she vacuumed the house, for example, she would tell the baby she was carrying on her back about what she was doing, that the noise was made by the motor inside the vacuum cleaner, which was electrical and turned very fast, that the air it blew through made a lot of noise, and so on…

One could imagine her manner being cheerful and natural – not 'schoolmarmish', giving stern lectures, but rather 'Hey, this is interesting!' If you find car trips or shopping with little children rather boring at times, then perhaps this kind of chatter will make it more fun for both of you.

In our family we've gone onto the next problem now – how to stop a four-year-old from talking all the time! But at least he does it well!

The rats were willing to work very hard at lever-pressing to keep the movie in view, leading us to *principle one*: intelligent creatures, like rats (and children), like to have something interesting to do. This helps their brains to grow.

The researchers then put the rats in a different cage, with food and drink but no lever and no window. The rats were content for a little while but then started misbehaving! They chewed the walls, fought with each other, rubbed their fur off, and were generally bad rats! This leads us to *principle two*: intelligent creatures, like rats (and children), will do anything to keep from being bored including things we could call silly or destructive.

Finally, the researchers really got nasty. They tried a cage with food and drink, and with little wires placed across the floor and attached to a battery. Every now and then a shock was sent through the wires, enough to give the little creatures a real start but not to injure them. (You see now why they didn't use children.)

Finally, the exciting moment arrived. The rats were taken out of the cages and given a choice of which they would prefer to go back into. Perhaps, you the reader, could make a guess as to which was the rats' first choice, second choice, and so on? Here they are again:

cage with food, drink and movies;
cage with food and drink;
cage, with food, drink and unexpected shocks.

Have you guessed? Well, the rats preferred the movies best of all. If you didn't guess that one...back to the start of the book! The second choice was the really interesting one: they preferred the cage with shocks to the one with only food and drink. This leads us to *principle three*, an important principle indeed for children: intelligent creatures, like rats (and children), would rather have bad things happening than nothing at all.

Or, in other words, any stimulation or excitement is better than none, even if it's somewhat painful.

In child terms, if a child has to choose between being ignored and being scolded or even smacked, which do you think he'll prefer? Which do your children choose? Of course, if positive attention is available, at least once or twice a day, then neither of the above will be so appealing.

I'll conclude this chapter with one more story – this time about children. You are smarter than children or rats so it won't need explaining!

An up-and-coming young couple had two boys, aged nine and eleven. The boys had a playroom under the house with a billiard table, a refrigerator full of soft drinks, a record player (video games hadn't been invented at that stage, or they would have had one of those, too), and so on.

However, the parents found that, despite the facilities provided, the boys were always fighting; it was even embarrassing to have guests to dinner. They finally took the boys to a behavioural clinic to seek the help of psychologists. The psychologists said to the parents, 'Well, we mostly know about rats, but we're willing to come over and have a look'. The arrangements were made. The parents thought it a little odd, but were keen to solve the problem that was badly affecting their social life.

The psychologists came in a team and installed themselves around the house with notepads and stopwatches. It was the evening of a cocktail party, so some of the psychologists stayed upstairs (where the adults were) and some were with the boys downstairs (sitting silently taking detailed notes). At about seven o'clock the upstairs observers noted the mother glancing downwards and then across at her husband. Simultaneously, the observers downstairs had noted that the boys, having played with the various games and toys, had begun to fight. The fighting was rather unusual, though – it had more the look of a stage fight or a kind of a dance. The noise, however, was very fight-like!

The observers in the basement then saw the father appear on the stairs and, having been told by the psychologists to act normally, not an easy thing to do, begin to berate the boys for being disruptive.

The psychologists scribbled furiously: they had noticed a unique thing, something they had never seen in rats. The boys listened to their father shouting and looked suitably chastised, except for a small and curious twist about the mouth – an expression which has become famous. Psychologists call it 'the Mona Lisa smile'...

Child psychologists now realise that this half-smile is a secret message, which means, 'Well, I should be feeling bad, and I'm trying hard to look remorseful but, you know, I'm kind of enjoying this!' Parents have never really figured this out but they react to it unknowingly with that famous parent sentence, 'Wipe that smile off your face when I'm talking to you!'

Meanwhile, back in the basement, the boys were getting more attention from Dad than they had received all day and had to struggle hard not to show their pleasure.

The psychologists went back to their laboratory, prepared a detailed report and met with the parents to tell them what you have probably already guessed: 'You're too busy with your social life; the boys need more attention. They like their Dad because boys of this age want to learn how to be a man, and so they have found the one thing that they know will bring their Dad into the picture: fighting.'

The psychologists were right, but they didn't understand parents very well. The parents' reply was, 'What a load of rubbish. How could children possibly like being told off?' The parents, you see, didn't know about the rats and the electric shocks, let alone the Mona Lisa smile.

The parents took their boys off to a psychiatrist, who analysed their dreams for two years, then gave up and Dad took them to play golf with him, which of course cured them! We can easily summarise the above.

Children play up because they're bored.
Is there something you could do to give them more stimulation – have their friends over, join a play group, get toys from a toy library, have a large box of bits and pieces for imaginary play so that they, and you, don't feel 'caged in'?

Children play up because they feel unwanted.
Can you spend a little time giving full, positive attention and physical contact? And are you relaxed and happy enough to give them a secure feeling?

Children play up because it gets them noticed.
Watch for the Mona Lisa smile, a sign that some attention is needed for doing the right thing.

FATHERING – DOING THINGS TOGETHER

When our son was small we lived on a quiet country road, half a kilometre from the post office and general store. It was a nice walk to get the mail, on a sunny morning, and took ten minutes there and back. Unless you took a two-year-old kid along! Two-year-old kids do not think like adults – they do not know the meaning of 'long term goals'. They don't even have 'application to the task in hand'. Anything but. Each step of the way has to be the subject of intense negotiations! 'I wanna play inna pretty green water!'

Once, out of sheer dedication to science, I tried something out. I completely gave in, and let 'the kid' investigate every drain, ditch, dead worm, puddle and rock that he wanted to, along the way. (If early influences determine eventual careers – Rohan will be something big in sewerage.) Anyhow, to cut a (very) long story short, it took two and half hours! After a while, I even started to enjoy it!

It's very clear from everything we know about families, that kids – especially boys – get a lot out of being around fathers. Something different and complementary to what mothers provide takes place at these times. And for the most part, being with fathers means 'doing things together'. It's not like in the movies and shows like *The Waltons*. In the Waltons family they sit down, and have 'heart-to-heart talks'. Maybe this happens in the old U. S. of A., and good luck to them, but most people go kind of catatonic if they are sat face to face like that. Of the people I spoke to, those who got on well with their Dads did some talking and listening – but it was carefully concealed amidst activity, with trust and self disclosure growing gradually – while on the surface just loading the wood, working on the car, getting in the sheep.

You'll notice some of these are rural pursuits. The city doesn't lend itself quite as much to doing things together – not so actively anyway. You can only take out the garbage so many times! City parents I talk to seem to get close to their kids while taxi-driving them between activities like athletics to ballet and back to piano. This is the time to actually ask how they are going, and draw them out a little, though you have to time it to the trip.

For fathers, doing stuff with your kids is vital. It allows closeness to just happen. Conversations wander into deeper realms. Things just kind of pop out unguarded, and an easy-going father can actually influence the direction of their own kids' lives – much better than leaving this all to Hollywood and peer groups.

When spending time with your kids:

1) Don't expect to actually achieve anything! Especially with small children (like going to the post office) the goal is no longer the goal. For example – if you are teaching them to use a screwdriver, you won't get the door hung in a great hurry. So let go of that one. They'll wander off in a while and you can make up for lost time.
2) Only do things with kids which you feel relaxed about. Their help in planting out spring seedlings will not give you an immaculate garden. You have to decide what you are doing – being with your kids, or getting the job done to your usual standards. If you try to do both you will experience a little frustration. If I'm writing on the computer, I can't stand to be interrupted. So I don't even try to involve my child.

3) Enjoy parenthood – it doesn't last! I was in my thirties when my son arrived, and so am mindful of parenthood being all too short. If he wanders by when I'm doing a job, I value the contact with him and like to see what I can teach him there and then. But not writing on the computer!

In conclusion – as a father you need to decide moment to moment what is more important to you, and it will sometimes be the kids, and sometimes not. One big plus is that kids tend to slow you down, and while slowed down, you start to rediscover little pleasures, which is the gift they bring. Time with kids is never wasted.

3

Curing by listening

How to help your child deal with an unkind world

Your child is upset. Something has happened at school or with another child or adult, and you don't know how to help. You would like your child to find a way of dealing with the problem so he or she will be less vulnerable. This chapter will show you how to help.

The world is sometimes an unfair and difficult place for kids and, much as we would like to, we parents can't smooth out all the bumps. In fact, we shouldn't, since it's through dealing with difficult people and situations that our children become mature and independent adults.

We'll look firstly at what not to say to kids when life is treating them badly: the kinds of statements that can put a wall between you and the child. Then you'll learn of a remarkable skill called 'active listening', which parents are finding is the most positive way they can help kids deal with life.

Many times, while growing up, children broach problems with their parents. They in fact ask for help. The way that parents react to these signals for help will either open up greater trust or put up a barrier that will be hard to take down. There are three ways that parents typically react, that cause the barriers to go up:

Patronising
'Oh, you poor thing. Here, let me fix it for you.'

Lecturing
'Well, you are stupid to have got into this mess, so I'll tell you what to do. Now, listen carefully to me...'

Distracting
'Oh well, never mind, let's go and play cricket.'

Which is your style? Do you rush to the rescue, or give wise advice, or change the subject?

We can take a closer look at each of these three styles.

Patronising

'How was your day?'

'Bad!'

'Oh, you poor thing. Come and tell me all about it.'

'We had this new teacher for maths. And I couldn't keep up.'

'Well, that's really awful. Do you want me to help you with the work after tea?'

'I didn't bring it home.'

'Perhaps I could ring the school tomorrow and talk to the principal?'

'Oh, well; I dunno...'

'I think it's best to get to the bottom of things before it gets worse, don't you?'

'Well, err...mmm.'

'I wouldn't want your education to suffer.'

'Uh-huh.'

Lecturing

'How was your day?'

'Bad!'

'Well, you're a fine one to complain. I'd love to be able to spend my day learning, having a nice easy time.'

'Well, we had a hard time. We've got this stupid new maths teacher...'

'Now don't you go talking about your teachers in that tone. If you paid a bit more attention you'd be better off, my boy. You think you should have everything on a plate!'

'Hmmm.'

Distracting

'How was your day?'

'Bad!'

'Oh, come on, it wasn't that bad was it? Have a sandwich?'

'Thanks. I'm a bit worried about maths...'

'Well, you're no Einstein, but neither are your Mum n' Dad. You go and put the TV on and don't let it get you down...'

'Uh huh.'

The three examples have several features in common: the parent does all the talking; the conversation stops pretty soon; the child doesn't get to talk over the real problem; the child's feelings get lost along the way; the parent 'solves' the problem – or thinks he has; the child says less and less.

Compare the previous responses with the following attitude.

Active listening

> 'How was your day?'
> 'Bad!'
> 'You look really unhappy. What went wrong?'
> 'Aw, we've got a new teacher for maths. He goes too fast.'
> 'You're worried that you won't be able to keep up?'
> 'Yes. I asked him to explain part of it and he just said to pay more attention.'
> 'Hmmm – How did you feel about that?'
> 'Really wild – the other kids all stirred me…but they're having trouble, too!'
> 'So you're angry that you got into trouble because you piped up first?'
> 'Yes, I don't like getting shown up in front of everyone.'
> 'What do you think you'll do?'
> 'I'm not sure, I suppose I could ask him again when the class is over.'
> 'You think that would work better?'
> 'Yes, then I wouldn't feel so embarrassed. And I think he's a bit nervous, too. Maybe that's why he rushes.'
> 'You can understand it from his point of view?'
> 'Yeah, I reckon he's just nervous of us.'
> 'No wonder, teaching smart kids like you!'
> 'Yeah!'

This, then, is active listening. In such cases parents are far from silent: they are interested, and show it by confirming the child's feelings and thoughts and by helping the child to think it through.

Using this approach, parents rarely give remedies or attempt to rescue ('I'll call the school');

they rarely advise ('you should ask for help');

they rarely distract the child from the problem ('Oh well, have a sandwich').

The skill of active listening takes some practice to acquire, and is taught in excellent courses such as those run by PARENT NETWORK throughout the UK.

Many parents have found active listening a great relief: they don't have to keep their child forever happy and they don't have to solve the child's problems for him. With active listening they can help the child, while leaving the responsibility, and pleasure, of a solution to the child. The trick is to ask yourself, ' Could my child benefit, in the long run, from solving this problem himself?' You can offer time, clarity and understanding so that a problem can be turned into a learning experience.

Sometimes parents must intervene, as the following story illustrates.

A friend of mine has a nine-year-old son who broke his leg and needed a plaster for some weeks. When the plaster was removed he was naturally shaky on his feet for a while. A physical education teacher at the primary school he attended had the class run round the oval and my friend's son came last, an embarrassment to him because he was a good runner. The teacher, without waiting for an explanation, made the boy run the oval again, but this time in his underwear only and in front of the rest of the class.

When the boy arrived home in tears and his parents learned of what had happened, they were so angry that they saw the school principal the same night and asked that the teacher be dismissed. The teacher was, in fact, transferred to another school, where we can only hope the same does not happen again.

This is a case in which parents must become involved and defend their children's rights because the children are powerless to defend themselves. In some cases, kids do not want our help – just our support. To get involved would be the wrong thing…

Janie is eight. As she rides home on the bus from school she notices something strange. The old man across the aisle has taken his penis out and is looking at her rather strangely. She goes to the front of the bus, gets off two stops early and runs home and tells Mum. She is frightened and embarrassed but nowhere near as upset as Mum now becomes. Mum calls the school principal. Next morning, at school a special assembly is held and Janie is brought to the front. The school is warned about what happened and the police visit the bus during the coming week.

None of this helps Janie at all. She is now embarrassed five times more than in the first place, and angry; too. All she wanted was to tell *somebody* and be reassured. But nobody asked her what she wanted. They took over.

'Just listening' is powerful medicine. If we can hold back from putting instant Band-Aids on every hurt, we can enter the deeper world of our children.

Mandy, aged six, was in a bad mood. In fact, she had been out of sorts for a few weeks. She was more argumentative with her younger brother and had started not wanting to go to playgroup in the mornings. Her mother decided to use 'active listening' to see if she could find the trouble. She asked Mandy, 'You look sad. Do you want to tell me about it?' Mandy came and sat on her lap but didn't talk much.

Next day, Mandy had to be stopped from fighting with her baby brother and was put in her room for a few minutes to cool off. Later that night, her Dad commented, 'You seem kind of cross at the moment.'

Mandy gave one piercing look at her Mum and burst into tears: 'They called me Yuk Face'. In the next ten minutes or so Mandy moved through anger and tears in succession, while her Mum resisted the urge to distract her or try and cheer her up. Mandy did indeed have a scar on her cheek, which would one day be healed with surgery, but for a while she would have to live with it.

When she had let out some of the bad feelings she'd collected from children at school, Mandy was much more peaceful. 'I'm not yukky, am I, Mummy?' Nope! You're terrific!

Sometimes children want you to do something – in which case they should ask straight out.

Jonathon, aged fourteen, hung around the kitchen for ages, looking very awkward. Finally he told Mum, not without embarrassment, that an older girl had asked him to a motel for the night with her! His mum had to battle hard not to start laying down the law. She said instead, 'Gee, what do you think you'll do? You sound like you're feeling pretty unsure.' 'Well, I don't know. Mum, would you forbid me to go? Please?'

Jonathon's Mum was very happy to forbid him to go. Jonathon was most relieved: he saved face at school and with the girl. Jonathon's mother told me later that she would have forbidden him to go but wanted him to make his decision, too. A brave lady!

4

Kids and emotions

What is really going on?

This is probably a good place to make a confession. The title of this book *The Secret of Happy Children* is a little idealistic!

In the adult world, no-one is ever, or would want to be – continually happy. So for our children, such an aim actually would be wrong. If you try to make kids happy all the time, you will actually make them and yourself quite miserable! What we really want is kids who can handle and move along through the many feelings that life brings…Joy is the goal, but being comfortable and experiencing all the emotions life brings is the way to get there most often.

A proper understanding of emotions has been missing (at least in our culture) until recently. We've only just escaped from the era of 'big boys don't cry', and 'it's not ladylike to get angry'. Few areas of understanding are as needed and helpful right now as getting back in touch with how feelings work. Luckily, the 'facts about feelings' are now available to help both us, and our kids, to find both the inner peace and vitality that make up emotional health.

What do we mean by emotions?

In their pure form, emotions are distinctive sets of body sensations, which we experience under specific situations. They range from subtle to very strong in intensity. They are constantly with us – flowing and merging together as we resolve each event in our life and move on. We are always feeling something – emotions are a symptom of being alive!

There are four basic emotions – *anger*, *fear*, *sadness* and *joy*. All other shades of feeling are a mix of these – like colours mixed from the primaries red, yellow and blue. There are thousands of combinations possible – like jealousy – a mixture of anger and fear; or nostalgia – a mixture of joy and sadness! We are such interesting creatures!

When our children are newly born, their emotions are only just beginning to take shape. Observant parents can watch babies in the early months developing separate and distinct expressions of how they are feeling – the shriek of fear, the tears of sadness, red-faced rage, and chortles of joy.

Infants are not inhibited – they *express* feelings naturally and easily, and as a result the negative emotions they experience rarely last for long. However, a child has to *learn* how to deal with feelings socially, and find constructive directions for the powerful energy that feelings give us. A child depends on us as parents for this information – luckily it isn't too hard to get this right – as we'll show. Understanding emotions – why we have them, how they can be best expressed, what to avoid – this information will give you a vastly better sense of how to handle children.

Why do we have emotions?

Sometimes you could almost wish you had no feelings – life would be easier to take. Especially the negative ones like anger or sadness, which cause so much pain. Why then did nature equip us with these highly charged states? Each has a big role to play – as you'll see.

Take anger first. Imagine a person who for some reason never feels anger. Somehow they were raised without a cross bone in their body! They are standing one day in the shopping centre car park. A car drives up and parks on their foot! Our super-accepting person would just stand there waiting until the driver did their shopping and came back!

Anger is what makes us stand up for ourselves. Without it we would be slaves, doormats, mice! (Even more than we are at present.) Anger is our instinct for freedom and self-preservation.

Fear is of definite value too. Why else do you drive on the correct side of the road? Fear keeps you from taking risks. If you don't believe fear is useful, recall the times when you've been a passenger in a car with a driver who seems to have no fear! Fear slows us down, forces us to stop and think and avoid danger – even when our conscious brain has not yet fathomed what that danger might be.

Sadness is the emotion that helps us to grieve – it literally washes us clean of the distress of losing something or someone from our life. The chemical changes which go with sadness help our brain to release the pain, and so move on to new life. Only by being sad can we 'let go' and so make new contact with people and life. So you can see that properly handled,

anger…….	keeps us free;
fear………	keeps us safe;
sadness…..	keeps us in contact with people and the world.

All three of these outcomes are central to our happiness. Joy, the fourth emotion, is what we start to experience when these needs are fulfilled.

We can teach children specifically how to understand and handle each of the three negative or balancing emotions. We'll now look at each in turn.

Teaching kids about anger

The immediate impulse that children have when they are angry is to hit out. This has a natural purpose, but must be modified somewhat if we are to get along in the world. Anger is the feeling that parents most often want to modify, so we'll tackle it first.

Whenever we intervene with children, our aim should be help them learn what will work and serve them well as adults. Think for a moment – what is an ideal way for an adult to handle anger? It comes down to a balance. A person who is being mistreated in some way needs to be able to say so out loud, with conviction, and to do so early on (before they feel or act violent.) Anger and violence are not the same thing. Violence is anger gone wrong.

An adult learns to moderate their anger so that it has impact, but does not do damage or become abusive. If our child shows too little anger, they may be seen as a wimp, and be pushed around or used by other kids. Too much anger makes them unpopular or even a bully. Getting this balance right is what our kids need to learn about – and it takes a few years of practice, starting from toddler age on.

To help kids be comfortable with anger:

1) Insist that they use words instead of actions to express anger. They have to say out loud that they are angry, and if possible why.
2) Help them to connect their feelings with reasons. Talk with them to check out what is behind their outburst. Young kids will sometimes need help to 'think back' to what went wrong.
   'Are you angry with Josh because he took your truck?'
   'Did you get sick of waiting for me to finish talking?'
   Soon they will be able to tell you what is wrong and why – instead of going straight to impulsive actions.
3) Let them know that feelings are heard, and accepted (but may not always change things).
   'You've got a right to be angry with me. I wasn't listening. I'm listening now.'
   or
   'I know you're tired of waiting in this shop, and so am I, but that's just how it is. What can you do to feel better instead of hassling your brother?'
4) Teach directly that hitting is not an acceptable way to handle anger. Confront this directly, give a negative consequence for each and every hitting instance, and insist that a child do what they should have done in the first place (usually use words)!
5) Help children to say what they DO want. Often they will start to whine and complain about what they don't want. They need your help to be more positive…
   'He hits me.'
   'Tell him very loud not to do that.'
   'Myra took my bike.'
   'Go and ask her if you can have it back now. Tell her it's yours and you want it.'

6) Show them by your own example. When it's all added up, they are more likely to do what you DO, than what you SAY. So be sure to role model what you want. When YOU are angry, say so, in a loud voice. Get angry and be loud early, before you are REALLY steamed up. Once it is dealt with, let go, so they will learn that anger can be expressed, and then is gone. Simply say the words often and easily:
'I'm angry!'
'You're crowding me!'
'Stop interrupting!'
'Don't touch my things!'
'I'm annoyed that you didn't keep our deal. What's going on?'

Kids learn far better about anger from a parent who is moderately expressive, than one who is always sweet, reasonable and contained. Kids need to see that parents are human too.

You can be very angry with kids without ever using abuse, or put-downs. Just stick to the direct expression of feelings and reasons. For kids, getting anger right takes a while. Be happy if your children are showing *some* signs of restraint – you will see them holding back from hitting another child or you, or saying out loud 'I'm angry'. Many adults haven't learnt these lessons yet, so you are making good progress.

Teaching kids about sadness

There has always been a folklore understanding of sadness – that it's good to have a cry when things become too much. Fighting against this has been the strait-laced Victorian notion of the stiff-upper lip, of 'being a man' or 'being strong'. Also in everyday useage amongst kids is the idea that you can cry too much, and that to do so is a bit suspect – there's a special name for this, being a 'cry baby'.

To cry sometimes is as necessary and as natural as breathing. Far from making you strong, not crying actually makes you uptight, you tend to live in the past and be hard to contact in the present, and fearful of other people's emotions or anything associated with death or loss. If you know how to cry and release sadness, you know you can handle anything.

It was discovered only this decade that when a person cries, their body releases chemicals of the endorphin family, which block pain receptors, and produce a healing anaesthesia through the worst of the anguish that loss sometimes brings. This chemical is present even in our tears themselves. It's closely related to, and as powerful as, morphine.

To help kids be comfortable with sadness

Sadness follows its own course without a lot of help. All we need to do is be present, calm ourselves down as we sit or stand with a child who cries. Sometimes they will want to press against us and be held, other times they will want to be separate.

If it feels right, you can give permission: 'It's okay to cry', 'It's really sad about Grandpa', 'I'm sad too'. You can explain slightly if a child is confused or awkward: 'Tony was a good friend of yours. He's worth feeling sad about', 'Sometimes crying feels awful, doesn't it?'

We once were at a friend's place. We were watching a great video movie called *Mask*. It had just ended, and everyone was enjoying being sad, in fact our hostess was sobbing loudly. Her three-year-old appeared at the door in pyjamas, came over to mum, put a tender hand, and said 'It's okay, let it all out!'

Helping children handle fear

Fear is something we all need. It's vitally important that children learn to freeze, and stop from running into danger. Also we want to know that they can run or jump quickly to avoid being hurt by a speeding car or a bicycle out of control veering their way on the footpath going to school. And in our urban world, to fear the over-friendly stranger or a person acting strangely is also vital.

On the other hand, being too afraid is a real handicap – children also need to be able to speak to adults, talk up at school and get their needs met, and join in socially. They need to see the world as a basically safe place, if handled properly. We'd like them to be brave enough to try new things – sports, exercise, creativity and so on.

Fear has two purposes. It focuses you. A snake rearing up in front of you on a bush track soon stops you being dreamy and careless. Fear also energises you. You will run faster and jump logs higher than you thought possible!

What kids need to learn in order to deal with fear is summed up in one word – think. We use our minds to sort out our fears. To plan for what we may need to do. When my job involved a lot of flying around the country, I found myself becoming more and more unhappy on planes. They felt unsafe – high up, bumping through clouds, wings flexing and so on. I had to check myself out – that no Australian jetliner had ever crashed, that plane travel is safer than road travel, that all around the world thousands of jets are routinely in the air all the time. And I found this worked. This is exactly the approach I take with kids.

Four basic hints for dealing with fears:

1) Be very matter of fact. Three- and four-year-old children often start to think about the wide world around them, and come up with lots of concerns – this stage is even known as the 'fearful fours' in some books. Talk it over with them, be patient but casual. Validate a child's intuition – they will often experience caution about people or places which will be well founded, though hard to explain at the time. Fear is a kind of radar, which has served the human race well through a dangerous past.
2) Talk fears over. If a child raises a realistic (if remote) fear, then explain the unlikelihood of it happening, but do figure out an action plan – figuring out with them what they would need to do to feel safe again.
3) If they raise an unrealistic fear, tell them so. Don't search under their bed for monsters, unless you live in the Komodo Islands or somesuch!
4) Underlying fears. If they are constantly fearful, use your listening skills to search out if there is something else that is troubling them, which they find hard to tell you.

Because of the different kinds of dangers facing children today, especially living in large impersonal cities, the KIDSCAPE Personal Safety

Programme has been introduced in thousands of schools throughout the UK. KIDSCAPE teaches children ways to stay safe from threats such as bullying, child abuse and abduction. KIDSCAPE teaches children to YELL, RUN, TELL and to get support from adults. Basically it teaches children that they have the right to feel safe all the time. (If only that were true for the whole world!) It skilfully avoids teaching younger children the specifics of sexual abuse – those experiencing it know these all too well and those who haven't been abused don't need to know. KIDSCAPE does not quiz or identify individual kids. It does teach children how to get support and advice from key adults, so that they know how to get help in case of danger. After KIDSCAPE has been introduced, the reported verifiable cases of abuse and bullying often increase dramatically. However, the incidence of reported child abuse and bullying cases then tend to fall because the children have told and because other children have managed to get help immediately or to prevent abuse happening in the first place. There have also been numerous cases of children escaping from abduction attempts and attributing their escapes to the KIDSCAPE Programme. If the KIDSCAPE Programme isn't in your child's school, ask why not!

Programmes such as KIDSCAPE are wonderful, but they never take away from adults the responsibility to protect children and care for them. Children have very limited power and it's up to parents to be alert, informed and watchful. And that we let our children know that they can tell us anything without fear.

In summary, kids need a little fear in their lives to protect them. They don't need overloading with adult fears – it's our job to take care of those. They need teaching how to think through danger situations, and one good way is to plan with them 'What would you do if…' in response to questions they ask, or dangers you want to prepare them for.

Rackets – when feelings get out of hand

We all have an intuitive sense that there is a difference between a real emotion, and one that is 'put on'. Children often get such a good reaction when they show a particular emotion, that they learn to run out that feeling whenever they want the desired effect. Each set of parents will have unique preferences for the feelings they most sympathise with. The child thus learns the emotion 'most likely to succeed'.

Each feeling has a 'phoney' counterpart, which psychotherapists refer to as 'racket feelings' (though we're looking for a kinder word).

Anger when put on as a racket is called a *tantrum*.

Sadness when put on as a racket is called *sulking*.

Fear when put on as a racket is called *shyness*.

These three emotions comprise some of the major challenges to parents of young kids, so let's look at practical approaches to each...

GETTING ON TOP OF TANTRUMS!

A child of eighteen months to two years old is just discovering that their wishes can conflict with the wishes of other people. Their feelings are so strong at discovering they are not God, that it can be quite upsetting for them. A parent has to be understanding and helpful with all these feelings, but still not give in to them. Early temper outbursts are a valuable chance to teach your child how to handle life with more good humour and flexibility. Naturally this might take a year or two to achieve! In fact, handling the full blown public tantrum is the gold medal challenge of parenthood!

So here's what to do when a tantrum happens:

1) CALM YOURSELF by noticing breathing and letting it be deeper and slower. Notice your muscles too, and let them go looser if you can. *Don't have a tantrum yourself!*

2) HELP YOUR CHILD by sitting or standing close with them, or even holding and comforting them if they will let you. (If they are thrashing about on the ground you might have to settle for just staying close and waiting patiently!) Don't smack them or yell at them – this just pumps more emotion back into them to erupt at another time. By staying calm and present, you are letting them know you still love them *and* that the world isn't going to end just because they can't have what they want.

   (If you're in a supermarket or street, where you feel embarrassed or exposed, you might want to take them outside or off to a quiet corner. At a friend's house, you might take (or carry!) them to another room to have a quiet talk.)

3) DON'T GIVE IN – whatever happens don't give them what they wanted as a result of them having a tantrum. If you do, they will still be doing it when they are nineteen!

4) TALK IT THROUGH When they have calmed down, and especially if they are three or older, speak to them about how that is not a good way to get what they want. Discuss how else could they get along in that situation? To take turns with the toy, to wait till you finish on the phone, and then you will play with them, and so on.

5) PREVENTION Most tantrums and scenes occur *when you are both getting overloaded.* You will come to know the signs that your child is becoming tired or hungry, or even unwell, and be willing to change your plans for that long shopping trip or visit to grandma's. We all need to be able to say – 'hang on, this is too much' and take a break. Over-achieving adults can learnt to be less 'driven' once they become parents, because little children can't stand the stresses we might put ourselves under.

Some children just have preferences – they like to fasten their own seatbelt, or put the video in the machine themselves. Or they like a certain daily or bedtime routine and need to stick to it to feel secure. Take this as a sign that life really is a bit much for them, and they need a quieter and more even tempo to their life.

By taking a bit of time to weather tantrums though to a calm resolution, you are developing a good humoured and philosophical child who can usually find a way to be happy and get along with others.

BEAN BAGGING – HOW TO STOP THE SULKS

It's like pre-scripted theatre: They sit in the bean bag, in the middle of the lounge. You can't miss them. They aren't hiding their anguish! They issue loud and heart-rending sighs. Their face would win an academy award for special effects, so that you can't as a parent ignore them, so you ask, 'What's the matter?' The answer is time honoured – 'Nothin''. And that's only round one!

Sulking is aimed at proving something – to get you to show by your efforts that you care. You prove you care by hovering and guessing. 'Is it the food?', 'Was it something someone said?', 'How are things at school?', 'Are you not feeling too good?'. 'Nope nuh uh-uh…'

Eventually they allow you to give them some sort of special treatment, but even then are not really right – just mollified temporarily, nursing deep existential hurt until the next time! You wonder if you are somehow deeply inadequate as a father or mother.

Enough! Sulking only works if parents feel guilty in the first place, and so the child has learned to exploit this guilt. Perhaps you woke one night in a daze when they were a baby, accidentally took off their clean nappy and put on a dirty one. Or you stuck them with the nappy pin and now they've got post-traumatic stress. Whatever you're feeling about, if it is in the past, forget it – your guilt won't help your kids.

If we give attention and love to a child who is sulking, they learn a simple equation – love comes through being miserable. If you want to be cared for, just collapse yourself and work up a negative attitude, and people will give you free attention. The problem with this is that the family is not the world. Sulks don't have a happy life.

I encounter lots of kids and adults who sulk. (Being a therapist means being a parent to lots of children of all ages.) Once upon a time I would have worked hard to win them over, please them, draw them out. I was the 'feel good man' (though on the inside increasingly tired and angry). Now I am much more effective in changing such patterns. If a child sulks around me, I let them know 'I care about you. I'd like to help. Think about what you really want. I'll be in the kitchen.' And I leave them. Usually they come along and get more direct, and then I'm happy to help. Sulking is boring when you don't have anyone to sulk at.

Here are five key beliefs for an anti-sulk campaign:

1) Everyone – child or adult – does know what they want. They just need to think about it until they are clear.
2) Children can learn to ask for what they want, directly, in words.
3) People *need* very little – food, shelter, air, affection, exercise.
4) All the rest are *wants*. And you don't always get what you want!
5) Whether you feel happy or unhappy doesn't affect the world one iota. You may as well be happy.

THE MYTH OF SHYNESS

Do you have a shy child in your family? Well, after you've read this, you may want to change that! You see, shyness is a myth. It's a trap that kids get caught in, and don't know how to get out of. And while shyness may be cute in a child, it is a real handicap in later life. For the truth is, shy people miss out.

So how do kids get to be shy, and how can we help them to be more outgoing? Shyness starts by a mixture of accident and conditioning. We all are caught unawares in social situations sometimes, and get tongue tied. This happens to kids too. I once saw a clown go up to a toddler at a show, bend down close, presumably to say hello, and the toddler was nearly scared out of its wits! Actor Robin Williams recounts taking a two-year-old to Disneyland, and finding the child was not at all keen to shake hands with Mickey Mouse. The reason was that from the child's perspective ol' Mickey looked like a eight-foot RAT!

It's our job as parents to get our kids past this stage. After all, the people you introduce your kids to shouldn't be either dangerous or scary – so there's no need to act as if they are.

Here are the steps:

1) Teach your children how to be sociable. This is very simple. When someone speaks to your child, or says hello, and you are around, explain to them that they should:
   look up at the person who has spoken to them;
   say hello and add the person's name.

You can introduce people, saying 'This is Peter, (or Dr Brown, or whoever), say hello to him, please!' The child looks up and says 'Hello Peter', and that's it! For kids under four, leave it at that. They should not be the centre of attention for more than a moment or two – or they will be pressured into being little performers. Saying hello and making eye contact is a good start.

2) Insist that they do it! Three-year-old Angela was considered by her parents to be very shy. They often had guests visiting, and although Angela was boisterous and talkative before, she would become coy, hide behind her mother's skirts, and generally be awkward when new people were around. This behaviour was extended to her meetings with other children.

Her parents talked with us, and decided on a course of action. They gave her clear instructions about how to look up and speak when spoken to. When a friend, who had often been before, came to visit, and Angie acted very shy instead of saying hello, they told her to go and stand in the corner and think until she was ready to get it right. (The 'corner' is a technique used by many parents now to help kids think a problem through – an alternative to smacks or yelling.) Angie stood in the corner, but made a fuss, and was taken to her room. (By this time her parents were glad it was an old friend, they had, and not some judgmental strangers.) It usually takes effort to break through a pattern the first time. When Angie quietened down, she was brought back to the corner. She immediately said 'I'm ready'. (She may be stubborn but not stupid.) She then came out, easy as pie, and said 'Hello Maggie' to the visitor, and ran off and played happily. Soon afterwards, she approached Maggie easily and showed her a toy and chatted. The problem hardly ever occurred again, and when it did a few seconds in the corner sorted it out. Angela went from being a shy child to an outgoing one in a matter of days.

The only reason shyness persists in the first place is that some adults give so much attention to it. They think it is cute, loveable, and endearing, and make a great show of 'drawing a child out'. The child gets more attention than they ever would for just being straightforward. They provide a conversation piece for adults who can't think of anything better to say!

The only times when kids should be scared of people are when you are not around, or when there is something amiss, e.g. an adult who is actually dangerous, drunk, or known or intuited by a child to be a sexual danger. These people should not be around your children in the first place. Watch out for extreme reactions in your kids, and as soon as possible find out the reason.

Outgoingness is really just a matter of getting started with people, being friendly and making a move – and then things flow easily. By teaching your child to say hello, to make eye contact and introduce themselves, they will make friends, enjoy people, and their skills will grow. They will have a more successful life in all sorts of ways – socially, at school, and in their career. Well worth sorting out early on.

HELLO SALLY!
HI!
HELLO PETULA!
Oh you poor thing, Petula- some cake'll cheer you up!
better find some for Sally too

5

The assertive parent

Firmness. Do it – now.

In my work with families, I'm always having my eyes opened in one way or another. One of the first big surprises was to discover that some of the most stable and happy children were being brought up by incredibly harsh (to my way of thinking) parents. The secret seemed to be that these parents were hard but predictable – so consistent that their children knew exactly what the rules were and how to stay out of trouble. Because of this, they received punishment very rarely.

Most importantly, perhaps, these children knew that they were loved and valued because they were told so. Rejection was never a possibility: these kids would have sometimes been afraid, but never terrified and never made to feel abandoned. In brief, there were strong rules plus positive affection. If there had been one without the other I don't think it would have succeeded.

In contrast to these hard-but-fair families, I saw far more children who got away with remarkable misbehaviour but were still miserable. Clearly, these children were looking for someone to put the brakes on them, and their parents misunderstood the signals. They thought the children wanted more room and more freedom, but the opposite was true.

The need for limits is one of the secrets that parents need to know about. When social workers place a child in a foster home, after that child's own home has disintegrated, they have learned to warn the foster parents: 'The child may settle in easily but, more probably, he will play up a great deal in the first three months to test out you and your family unit – to see if it is strong enough to hold him. He will want to know if your marriage, your mental health, your affection and your discipline are strong enough. *Then* he can relax and begin to grow again. In short, he wants to know that this family will not break like the old one, and will test it to see!'

Fostering is the extreme example. But all children are the same: they need to know that someone is going to stop them.

We know from research that there are three main styles of parental response to children's playing up: aggressive, passive and assertive.

Aggressive parents use attack, either in words or action, to put their children down. Passive parents allow children to 'walk over' them and only regain control when it's 'the last straw' – and then by unexpected outbursts. Assertive parents are quite different. Let me explain the three to you in more detail.

The aggressive parent

Aggressive parents are angry with their children nearly all the time. Usually their anger is not a result of the child's behaviour at all. The parents may perhaps be resenting their marriage, their jobs, the human race, or the fact that they're parents and don't want to be (which is no fault of the children). They let out this tension by putting the children down.

Some children deal with this in a very interesting way. They realise that this is a kind of love, reasoning thus: 'At least they're interested enough to yell at me, and they yell loudly so they must care a lot!' The child may even yell back (to return the love), and soon parent and child are relating by fighting. Whole families can adopt this style, using what to an outsider looks like a dangerous free-for-all but is actually a kind of intimacy which all the participants would miss if it weren't going on.

Other children, sensing that the put-downs are really destructive in intent, become withdrawn and disturbed or, as we have seen, try to live up to the prediction and become the pest or the tramp they are being told they are.

As far as obedience is concerned, aggressive parents do get results, based on fear. However, they also get rebellion: many a bullying parent has one day faced a teenager big enough to hit back, and himself taken a beating. Aggressive parents end up with children who are either frightened and intimidated or rebellious and defiant – or a mixture of both!

The passive parent

Passive parents are everywhere! Let me use an extreme example to illustrate what passive parenting is like.

I once interviewed a young mother who complained about her child's disobedience. This was quite a common complaint but there were one or two unusual things that caught my notice. Most parents bring the child with them to see me. In fact, many would like to drop them off, saying, 'Here, you fix her!' This mother had not brought her child 'for fear of upsetting her' and had not told her husband either.

As we talked, she poured out details of the child's behaviour, obviously relieving herself of enormous worry and tension by putting it into words. She seemed so keen to unburden herself that it was a good half hour before I needed to speak. I asked how she dealt with disobedience and she replied that she was very firm but the child simply did not obey. I asked her to bring the child next time and show me.

The child was very co-operative and lived up to our expectations. After a few minutes 'casing the joint', she set about dismantling my telephone and curtains. I asked the mother to show me how she would stop the child. She immediately dropped her voice and murmured in soft, cautious tones, 'Melissa darling, how about stopping that?'

Naturally, there was no change. 'Please, love, come here, there's a good girl.'

I liked and respected this lady: she was an involved parent and wanted to do what was best for her child. However, her idea of firmness and mine were very different.

Some 'assertiveness training' was tried, and some help to trace and change the causes of her timidity: Melissa soon ceased to be the power in the family!

Good behaviour in children is required not as a whim of parents but to make practical living easier. Unlike parents of the Victorian era, we do not need pointless obedience, such as brushing one's hair before sitting down for tea or eating one's food in alphabetical order! We ask kids to co-operate so as to make life easier: 'Change before you go out and play', 'Stop hitting Susan!'

Therefore, when a child does not co-operate, the parents find their life inconvenienced. Soft parents will soon find they are being given the run-around. However much they want to give in and not inhibit little Damian's creativity, these parents find they are very angry and tired of the troubles this causes, and attempt to restore order. It may be after an hour of disobedience or a long week of repeated trouble but, whenever it happens, the parents suddenly will brook no more. Feeling very steamed up, they lash out and discipline the child in a way, and with a feeling, that they and the child know is somewhat out of control.

It will come as no surprise to you that parents who injure children are very often from this category: shy, timid parents who finally blow up after a lot of simmering. If you ever feel that you are a danger to your child's safety or your own when you 'blow up', then be sure to read Chapter 8 of this book to find out more about self-care.

As I write this, I'm feeling a lot of concern that you, the reader, may be feeling bad, recognising yourself in some of the above. If you have this pattern in your relationship with your child – back down, back, down, back down, blow up – then you need to know a couple of things.

- About a third of parents experience this pattern, especially when they have young children, and are just beginning to gain experience in parenting.
- It is not a big problem, just a misdirection of your energies and can be remedied.

So aggressive and passive parenting don't work – what's left? Finally (with a trumpet fanfare!) we announce the assertive parent.

Assertive parents are clear, firm, determined and, on the inside, confident and relaxed. Their children learn that what Mum or Dad says goes but, at the same time, that they will not be treated with put-downs or humiliation.

Assertiveness is not something you see every day and so you may not have a lot of examples to copy from. If your parents were aggressive, then it may be particularly hard for you to be assertive. The important thing is to see assertiveness as a skill, not something that you are born with. This means that you may take time to learn it. There's still hope!

The first part of assertiveness is on the inside of you, in your attitudes. Have a look at these scales.

'Mush' parents devalue themselves	**'Firm' parents decide they matter too**
• I come last in the family.	• I'm as important as the rest of the family.
• I have to keep the kids happy all the time or I'm a bad parent.	• The children are important, but they have to fit in with others, too.
• I mustn't frustrate their natural creativity.	• Frustration is part of growing up: the kids will often not get their way.
• I'm not much, really, but my kids might be someone someday.	• I need to be happy and healthy to be a good parent – I have to do things for myself, too.
• My spouse matters but not as much as the kids.	• My partner and our marriage are very important. The kids come (a close) second.
• Life is a bit of a struggle.	• Life is challenging but fun.
• I just want to keep the peace; I give in to the kids for the sake of some peace and quiet. Pity it doesn't last long.	• Sometimes I'm tired, but I have to teach the kids that I'm in charge. It's easier in the long run if they know where they stand.

The second part of assertiveness lies in action: what you actually do. Here is how to get good behaviour from a child who is used to disobeying or delaying.

Be clear in your own mind. It's not a request, it's not open to debate: it's a demand which you have a right to make, and the child will benefit from learning to carry it out.

Make good contact. Stop what you are doing, go up close to the child and get him to look at you. Don't give the instruction until he looks at you.

Be clear. Say, 'I want you to...now. Do you understand?' Make sure you get a 'yes' or 'no' answer.

If they do not obey, repeat the command. Do not discuss, reason, get angry or scared. Breathe slowly and deeply so that you become calmer. What you are signalling to the child is that you are willing to persist on this one and not even get upset about it. This is the key step, and what matters most is what you *don't do*. You don't enter into debate or argument, you don't get heated, you simply repeat the demand to the child.

Stay close if there is any chance that the child will not carry out the task fully. When the task is completed (say, putting away toys), then don't make much of this either. Simply say, 'Good,' and smile briefly!

This sequence is a retraining procedure. It may well be time-consuming the first couple of times, so that you'll think, 'Boy, it's easier for me to put the toys away!' But the time invested here will be repaid a thousandfold.

The trick is simply to persist. When the child discovers that you do not give up, give an entertaining minor nervous breakdown, or get sidetracked, then he simply gives in.

You will find that you soon develop a tone of voice and a posture that says 'I mean business' to your child. It's completely different from the voice that you use to discuss, tease, praise or play with your child. The child will recognise it as the voice that means 'Do it now!' And they do! It's a great feeling!

ATTEN-
SHUN!
Pick up
toys!

Once they've cottoned on to assertive parenting, it's amazing to look back at how you used to make things hard for yourself. For example, here is the great British bedtime drama. Names have been changed to protect the innocent!

It's nearly Cheryl's bedtime. Cheryl is four (or seven or eleven) years old.

Mum	**Child (to herself)**
It's nearly bedtime, Cheryl. Better start packing up!	*She said 'nearly – that means 'not yet'.*
Are you packing up your toys?	*Some chance!*
You know how tired you get in the mornings, dear…	*Mum's using reasoning with me – that means she's scared of me. Anyhow, morning is years away still.*
Come on, Cheryl, you don't want to cause another fuss, do you?	*Yep.*
Look, I'll help you put the dolls away.	*Goody! Mummy's gonna play with me!*
Hey, put those toys back. I just packed them away.	*Catch me!*
Cheryl, do you want me to get really cross?	*Yes! It's exciting.*
You're a naughty, naughty child.	*I suppose I am. I don't know why, but I really enjoy these fights. They really get Mum involved.*

The child's answers are, of course, unspoken. If Mum heard them she might not have been so willing to play along. The same sequence occurs in many situations. The main steps are:

- the parents fear conflict: they sound reluctant and hopeless when they first 'ask' the child to co-operate;
- they use reasoning and argument, not seeing that this is being used by the child to 'buy time';
- they give a lot of attention to struggling with the child, who enjoys the control and interest of having a big person on a string;
- the parents become fed up and crack down with more emotion and put-downs than they really wanted to use.

It's painful, especially if it happens every day. Thank goodness there's a way out.

One way to be angry and relaxed at the same time – pretend! One day when I was about thirteen, our science teacher was called out of the room. Soon we had out the squeeze bottles of distilled water and were re-enacting *High Noon* from behind the benches.

Although normally a timid child, I had got myself out to the front of the lab and was blazing away at the others, when suddenly their faces changed and they went still. A roar came from behind me and the teacher was back amongst us in a fury!

I was back in my desk almost by magic and didn't dare to even look up from my book. When I did, an amazing thing met my eye. The teacher was looking out over the silent class, grinning from ear to ear. I realised that he had been *acting* angry, and was amused by the instant results he had achieved as a result.

This was all new to me. I knew adults who got angry and went out of control, and others who got scared of their own anger, so that it came out all uneven. I decided that I liked this new kind better but that I'd stay in my place in future.

gives positive strokes

is not threatened by conflict

makes clear, firm requests and demands

negotiates more as children become older and more capable

sets rules and carries out the consequences

uses guilt, sickness, etc. to get child to behave

compares child with others, etc.

uses put-downs to make children behave

shouts at children

hits child angrily

withdraws totally

gives in to all child's demands

allows child to misbehave

Here are the four basic choices mothers and fathers have in dealing with children – don't use this chart to make yourself feel guilty!
Use it to remind yourself – 'I have a choice.'

The whole human race has been working out the discipline question for the last thirty to forty years, so you're not alone. Until this century, children weren't much of a problem: two-thirds of them died; the remainder were seen as of little consequence unless they got to their teens and then they were classed as adults. Violence was the standard means of control. These were the days when seven-year-olds were sent down unventilated mines or stood at factory machines for ten-hour days. Childhood is looking up.

In the fifties and sixties came the great era of letting children be people. Like all new movements, the pendulum swung a little too far, so that youngsters found themselves with the troublesome burden of being the most important people in the whole family. Needless to say, this wasn't very good for them either. Finally, the pendulum is swinging in to the middle. We are learning to give both soft love and tough love, and our kids are starting to show balance.

So, that's the story on assertive parenting. It starts with the decision that you as a parent have rights, and that your child needs your control (even though he or she may not agree). It ends with a much quieter life for everyone, and a lot more time for fun.

FATHERING – BACKING UP YOUR PARTNER

Many things in life are more easily done with someone else as backup, and one of those things is raising kids.

There's no doubt that handling kids takes determination, grit and purpose in order to get them back into line. Nothing feels better at these times than knowing you have the backup of your spouse.

Most people get a little shy of backup for a time, because they want to avoid the old way of doing things. What was the old way? It can be summed up in one sentence – Wait till your father gets home! This was not a fun arrangement – Mum alone and overwhelmed, drops the disciplinary role onto Dad, who, when he comes home just wants to relax, but ends up being the bad guy to the kids, who then get away with murder over Mum when he's gone again, and so on.

Backup is important, but it has to be done properly. There is one simple rule: when you back someone up, you don't need to take over.

Relationships are simpler if people deal with each other directly. Whenever communication becomes three-handed, it gets confused. Here is an example of how to stay straight…

Peter, aged thirteen, is hassling with Marjorie, his Mum, about putting out dirty clothes to be washed. He gets louder and begins to swear, and is talking too aggressively. His father overhears this, and walks in. He tells Peter 'Hey! You need to use a normal voice and sort this out with your mother now'. He catches Peter's eye. 'Right?' 'Mmm'. Dad then walks off, but stays within earshot. Peter then has to continue and solve the problem about the clothes.

The principle is this – a child who is dealing with their mother over something has to complete that process with Mum. Where a father comes in is to ensure that the child is respectful and gets on with it. In this way everything is kept simple.

The need for backup can occur when dealing with both girls and boys. However, boys especially seem at certain ages to go in for concerted limit testing – and it's handy to have Dad to 'bring on the cavalry'. But backing up should be available both ways. Both parents have to strike a balance of firmness and kindness too. You can't 'make up for' another parent's hardness or softness – each has to be a rounded person to the child. Another old way that seems to have been incredibly common thirty years ago was the hard parent/soft parent combination – where one parent tried to make up for the other's harshness. This doesn't work too well, since the child doesn't experience either parent being balanced.

Like everything else in parenting, you'll find a way that suits you. You'll know you're getting it right when your child says 'That's not fair! You're both against me!' – but doesn't seem too put out about it most of the time!

KIDS AND HOUSEWORK – HOW TO TEACH RESPONSIBILITY

Here is a neat way to reduce the housework you have to do, and help your kids get ready for adult life – all at the same time!

Kids today have it very easy. We are often amazed to hear of young adults – in their twenties – living at home, being cooked for and having their laundry done by their ageing parents! A lot of kids don't grow up (that is, they don't take responsibility for their own care and feeding) until they are in their early twenties. This is especially true of young men. Perhaps you are married to one!

All around the world, from Nepal to New Guinea to Nicaragua, it's normal for young children to have responsibilities. They are usually under watchful adult care, (not neglected like many affluent western children), but they have a daily round of chores, which they carry out quite cheerfully and with obvious pride. There is time for play, but this is incidental. The result of this working childhood is that in almost every other culture of the world, childhood flows smoothly and easily into adult life. How did we ever get the idea that childhood is a 'waiting room' before life begins?

Can we do a better job of helping our kids get ready for self-sufficiency in adulthood? Of course – and one way is by giving them work to do. You can start very early, from 18 months to 2 years, when kids can have a small daily task. Make this their special task which no-one else ever does.

The tasks increase month by month. Choose tasks which are regular and easy, involving self-care, and some which contribute to the overall family welfare. For instance by three they can set the table, and always take their own dishes back to the sink. As they get older you will easily be able to think of tasks which you can add on. Remind them, and follow up on them, and in time expect them to simply remember. Give praise and be proud of them, but don't go overboard – this is no big deal, just what is expected.

Much is made these days of self-esteem and the importance of praising and valuing kids and their efforts. However it's also important to remember that real self-esteem comes from contributing. Without knowing their place, and having a contribution, kids may get a kind of 'Young Talent' self-image – a ballooned idea of themselves which the big world away from a doting Mum and Dad will be sure to deflate.

This casual, graduated approach makes later stages much easier. Teenagers who have been helping out for as long as they can remember will not have the same resistance to pulling their weight – it will simply be routine. You're aiming for a young person who by the age of eighteen is making a contribution to the running of the household close to that of either adult parent. Cooking at least one family meal per week, being responsible for some other areas of family care. If sharing tasks between children, give them a mixture of the ones they like, and enjoy, but also a proportion that are not pleasant. Again you are aiming to be realistic – just as in adult life.

What about study? Some adjustment may have to be made at times of exam pressure. But by and large, study and homework are simply their 'day jobs', and shouldn't prevent them from making a contribution at home.

Remember you are aiming for competence in all the basic areas of life – cooking, cleaning, laundry, care of animals, budgeting, time-management, as well as negotiation and teamwork! When your youngsters leave home, they'll do so fully equipped to look after themselves. In fact they'll probably leave sooner to escape all the work!

6

Family shape

Dad? Who's Dad?

What comes into your mind when you hear the word, 'family'? Older people would conjure up a gathering of thirty or forty people – aunts, uncles, cousins and others. Relatives who very likely lived in the same district and got together many times a year, if not weekly for Sunday dinner.

What we have at the moment are not families at all. We haven't had real families since the car was invented, and we became dispersed. The 'two parent, three kids and golden Labrador' family is only a piece of family – and that's why it doesn't work very well.

What's more, the picture above is changing too. The *average* family is now often either a single-parent family, or a recombined family with only one of the child's parents and a new Dad or Mum, probably with their kids. This isn't necessarily a bad thing, but it is making life very different.

How does all this affect your children? Well, we have discovered that the shape of your family is very important, and you can alter its shape to make it a good place to be. Here is the Steve Biddulph plan for government policy-making on families! Let's use an example. Some people blamed all social ills on family breakdown:

'Where are you off to, young Merv?'

'Down to the football riots, Mum!'

'Well, don't be late home!'

Superficially, this is true, but what causes the families to break down? Have you ever seen the places where football hoodlums grow up? Or living conditions in Ulster or Soweto?

Income levels are important to start with. Below certain standards of 'liveability', no one can raise happy children. Above a certain point, though, the need changes from material to human resources. Education, the development of community, ways to belong and participate and work together with others, emerge as the strongest needs for healthy family life.

This, in money terms, is very cheap. A friend of mine organises self-help groups for people who've had breakdowns. If he keeps two people per year out of hospital, he pays for his own salary. In fact, he achieves vastly more than that.

For thousands of years people lived in villages or small towns. When modern cities began to appear, about 200 years ago, people still lived pretty much in the same neighbourhood as all their relatives. So the family unit looked something like the following illustration.

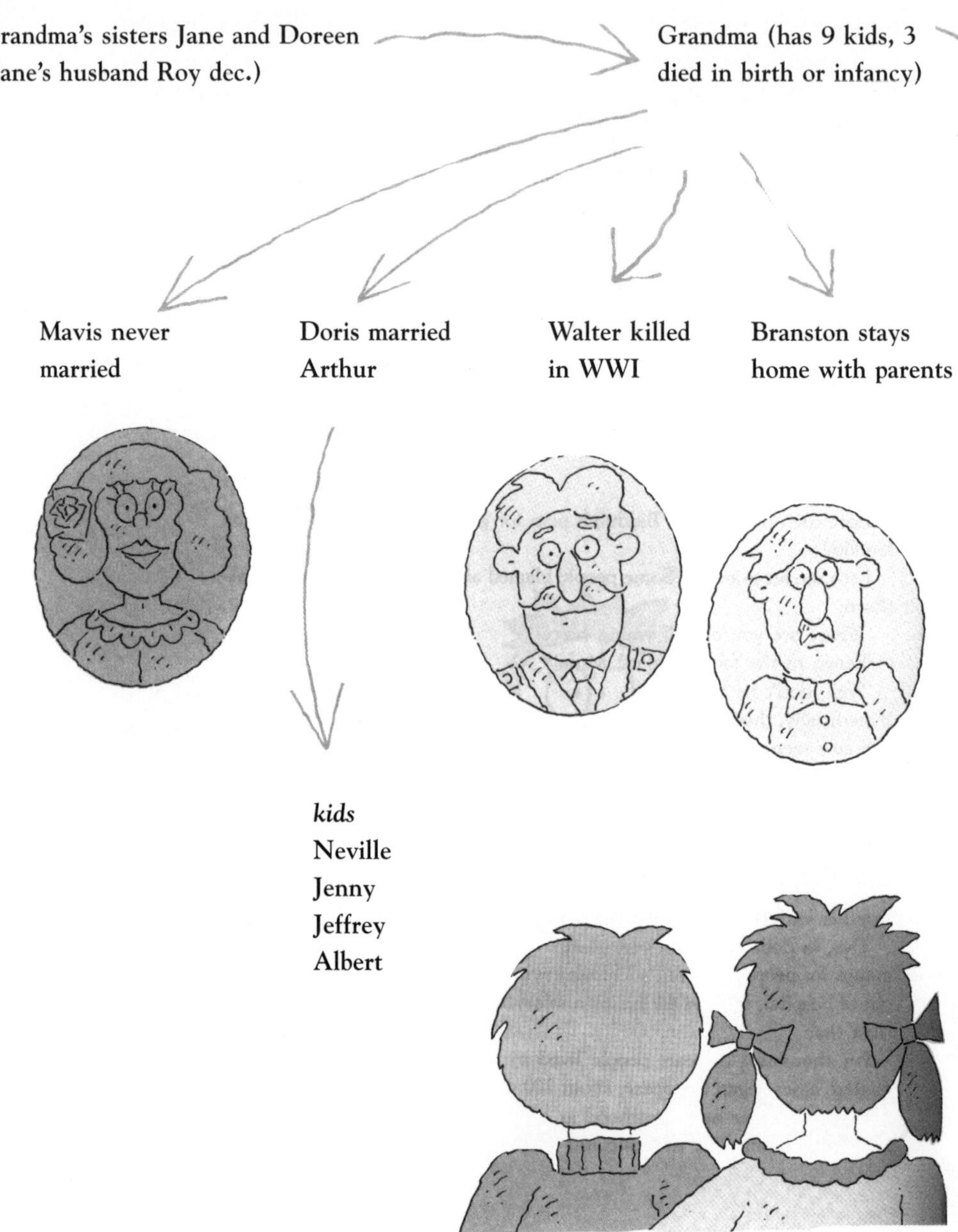
Grandma's sisters Jane and Doreen
(Jane's husband Roy dec.)
Grandma (has 9 kids, 3
died in birth or infancy)
Mavis never
married
Doris married
Arthur
Walter killed
in WWI
Branston stays
home with parents
kids
Neville
Jenny
Jeffrey
Albert

Grandpa
(helped)
Grandpa's brother
Cheswick (wife Enid dec.)
Enid married
Len (died WWI)
Wilfred
married
Naomi
kids
Angus
kids
Sophie
Emma
Faith
Hope
Desmond

As you can see, it's quite a gathering of people. And although times were hard, with people dying in wars and a lot of deaths in childbirth or infancy, this extended family unit was very supportive. For example:

> *Mavis (who stayed single) loves kids, and so often has little Jenny to stay with her. This is good for Doris, with the three boys. Doris is often unwell and Mavis cooks and helps clean once or twice a week.*
>
> *Enid's husband, Len, died in the war. Angus was born in 1920, which could have caused a few problems, considering the war ended in 1918, but, since Enid moved in with Wilf and Naomi, no one outside the family needed to know!*
>
> *Grandpa is a little over the hill and keeps waking up thinking the Boers are coming, but, luckily, Branston, the youngest son, is staying on at home and looking after the farm.*
>
> *Wilfred doesn't like children and is often away, but Arthur likes children and so takes the boys fishing, playing cricket, and so on – so they don't miss out too badly.*

The 24 people in this hypothetical family don't actually live together (there are six households in all) but it would be a rare week that they didn't all see each other at some time or other. The family unit was able to withstand wars, illness, deaths, Enid's 'flying Scotsman' and various failings and foibles; and everyone was guaranteed a place and some security.

It was a hard time, but there was less uncertainty. For parents, this had definite advantages. Right was right and wrong was wrong. If you weren't everything your children needed, there were others to step in. You were never alone – there was plenty of advice, help and example. You got lots of practice with other people's children and your younger brothers and sisters before you started on your own. You could even choose not to have kids at all and still not be too lonely.

There were lots of restrictions and demands, too, and not many of us would go back, even if we could, to that kind of extended family. But the good things that were there for parents – could we ever get those back? I think so, and would like to tell you how.

You don't have to be related – just committed!

Let's take the loneliest modern family: the single parent with one or two young children. (Some would argue that there is an even lonelier combination: the unhappily married family, the reason so many people go back to being single. Fair enough.)

What is missing?

The grandparents may not live close by; we move about so much these days.

There may not be other adults who are interested in the kids – the uncles and aunts.

There may be no father figure to play with and be a back-up in discipline and decision making (if you're a single Mum).

The girls at work
the teenage chap who mows the lawn
this young lady you've been seeing a lot of,
and her kids. This nice bloke you met at a barbecue
and his kids, the fellas up the street who take the
kids to the cricket, the old lady, next door neighbours

"The Extended Family of the Future!"

There may be no woman to handle 'girl's stuff, go to the school during the day to see teachers, or share in discipline and decision making (if you're a single Dad).

There may not be other kids to play with or safe places outside the house or flat for the kids to go.

When really hard things happen there's no-one to talk to that you can really trust or who will help you materially, just because you're 'family'.

But the fact that all these things are not available doesn't mean that they may not be found. For instance, old people sometimes really like kids. Might it be possible to find some 'grandpersons' who live nearby, who could become part of your family? (You paint their ceiling, they mind your kids!)

There are other single parents, or not-single parents, dying of loneliness very close to you. Do you think people really go to Tupperware parties to buy plastic bowls? They go for something to do, and someone to talk to. Other parents are dying to talk to you.

You can find out about groups that have been started in the community. Playgroups are really just like Sunday afternoon at Grandma's place, where kids can play and parents can talk and join in. Courses run by adult education centres are good meeting places and very friendly. Schools, playgroups, infant health centres, clinics, the hairdresser, sports clubs, churches – choose whatever suits your style.

It's very hard work, and if you move you have to start all over again. Nonetheless, you can actually make yourself an extended family if not for your own sake, then for your children's.

There's another part of family shape that is very important, even is your family is the official two adults and two-and-a-bit kids.

When you started out as a couple it was simple. There were just the two of you, and you probably had a nice time.

Then, when kids were added in, it might have started to get complicated. Many families find themselves caught in one of these 'shapes':

You've probably experienced all three at some time. And with more kids, the combinations can get even tougher:

These are natural alignments for the family from time to time, but they are bad news if they become the normal shape of your family.

What we have found in hundreds of families seeking help is that *the closeness of the parent-couple is very important*. Kids seem to grow up most easily and happily when Mum and Dad are affectionate and interested in each other – to such a degree that the children could not come between them, even if they tried (which they do!).

One expert became famous for saying that the best sex education in the world was for Dad to give Mum a pinch as he walked past her in the kitchen, and for Mum to obviously enjoy it! All the rest, he said, was just so much plumbing! In the interests of non-sexism, I'm sure it would be just as good the other way round (Mum pinching Dad!)

Kids actually seem to gain reassurance from the fact that parents spend time together and they are not allowed to interrupt. If you haven't been in the habit of doing this (so that the kids have first call on you even when you are talking to your partner) – they you may find that it takes a while to break the pattern.

Problems seem to arise whenever:

- a parent frequently sides with a child against the other parent;
- a parent seeks affection and approval from a child, in preference to, or instead of, his or her spouse;
- a child is forced into a parent role too often, for example, having to care for other children or being part of decisions that are really parents' decisions.

I was enraged once to hear a well-meaning relative tell a nine-year-old boy, whose father had just died, that he would have to 'be a man now and take care of your mother'. Kids should be kids!

Every person is different and no advice can be completely right. All I can do is give you the general rules that we have found, and which may apply to you and your children.

DO NOT DISTURB
"they're making love"
DO NOT DISTURB
'OOOH'
AAH
'OOH'
"it's a kind of wrestling

- In a single-parent family, kids are much happier when their parent has a close, affectionate relationship with another adult. Whether it is their natural parent or not, or whether the other adult is the opposite sex or not, doesn't matter greatly; what matters is that their parent is happily matched.
- When parents are badly out of step with each other and seem to be in conflict all the time (not just the now-and-again conflicts that all couples have), then the children feel this acutely. The conflict cannot be hidden from the children, no matter what is done to conceal it. In fact, as long as parents do not act violently or cruelly or in ways that humiliate each other it's better that the children see the conflict out in the open, and realise that they are neither to blame nor going to suffer.
- A child is happier with a single parent than with two in an unhappy marriage. Staying together 'for the children's sake' when the marriage is making you miserable is a mistake.

A couple recently appeared in the Family Court to obtain a divorce. The man was ninety-one and his wife eighty-six.

The judge asked why they were getting divorced after all these years. They replied, as so many couples before had, 'We can't stand each other!'

'But why did you stay together all these years?' asked the Judge in dismay.

'Because,' said the couple, 'we wanted to wait until the children had died.'

BUT WHAT IF YOU'RE A SINGLE MUM?

Single parenthood has both advantages and difficulties. The advantages are that you don't have to put up with differing standards, conflicts between parents, and so on. You're the boss! Separated mothers have often told us that life is a lot smoother – for instance they just don't have the same 6 p.m. rush hour syndrome, as they did when a tired, hungry husband arrived home from work, and kids were disruptive and demanding. On the other hand, many things, like discipline, are harder to do by yourself. Let's look at this.

Sometimes as kids are growing up, it's necessary to 'lean on' them with a lot of force and persistence. You can see the need to bring them into line, for your sake and theirs, but it just gets tiring. At certain ages boys especially are hard for single mothers to manage. It seems to be a biological need for some boy children to experience strong conflict, and be firmly and frequently controlled until they learn to temper their strength and rebellion and so get along with other people. Put simply, they actually seem to want a fight, and only relax and let up when you give it to them. At times like these, a father would come in handy.

It seems that fathering, and mothering, are two different kinds of input, both of which kids need, to grow up well. If need be a mother *can* provide fathering, and a man can provide mothering. The lesson of the feminist era is clear – woman and men are not *so* different. A woman *can* do anything a man can, and vice versa (with some obvious biological exceptions!). The difference is though that a man will often find it easier, less against the grain, to be tough on kids.

A mother raising kids alone can muster this hardness, but it will take a lot of energy, because it draws on the male liking for combativeness, which she will not find so readily available. A single mother will need to practise, and acquire toughness, and at the same time not lose her compassion and peace-making skills.

Lots of single parents have told us that once they know this, it makes things less mystifying and overwhelming – they just learn to 'change gear'.

COUPLE TIME!
THE TEN MINUTES THAT CAN SAVE YOUR MARRIAGE

Would you like to turn the worst time of the day into the best time? Would you like to have romance, warmth, friendship and relaxation in your life – forever?! We can't offer a better start to these goals than the following ritual. Taken daily, or as needed – you can make evenings go well, and stay happily married. No kidding!

When you and/or your partner arrive home in the evening, you may have got into the habit of putting off relaxation until things were over with – meals, housework, kids, etc. This may work fine when the kids are little and in bed by seven. But not for long – as they get older, you wait longer to be together again. In the old days, husbands and wives were together more of the time, and got into a rhythm together. The widely differing tempo of our workdays apart means that when we come back together in the family home, we're spinning like tops at different speeds. So it's hard to feel connected. In fact many couples positively clash all night, only starting to synchronise late in the evening, if they have any energy or motivation left!!

Therefore we need to make sure that we DO get phased in together. The way to do this is as follows:

1) MEET! As soon as you are both home, sit down, and take a few minutes out together. And while you're doing this…
2) EAT!! Have some convenient but substantial snack food – salami, nuts, cheese, fruit, fruitcake, something with body in it to fill the hungry gap and give some instant energy. Next step is…
3) KIDS TO ONE SIDE! Children, who are often the only ones who do score any time and attention around teatime, have to stay out of the way. If they can do this in the room, fine – if not, send them out of the room. Their turn will come. Be tough on this one! It's only ten minutes.
4) DRINK. If you drink alcohol at all, make this the time for it. A single wine, beer or sherry together, with the snacks, will help you rapidly slip out of the day's tensions and let your body know this is winding down time.
5) TALK only if you want to. If you do, be sure to talk about good things. Avoid completely the old competition couples play – called 'Who Had The Worst Day?' Either talk positively, or sit quietly and enjoy just being there.

Soon you'll be settled enough to want to get on with the evening's activities – You can cook a more leisurely meal, since you are no longer desperately hungry, or be with the kids if you are the one who has been absent all day. You'll find that everything flows better because your whole rhythm – even down to your heartbeat – is more synchronised with your partner's.

This daily ritual is so simple, and yet its effect is profound. It saves marriages. It's as simple as that. Give it a go!

7

Ages and Stages

Do you mean this is normal?

Kids do change as they grow. What's right to say to a three-year-old could be wrong to say to a seven-year-old, and different again from what you would tell, or require of, a teenager. An idea of stages helps you to know what should be going on at a particular age, and how best to react.

The stages explained in this chapter are adapted from a book called *Self Esteem: A Family Affair*, by Jean Illsley-Clarke (not currently available in the UK). I've discussed them with thousands of parents and the most frequent response has been 'Aaaahhh! That's exactly right!' and, sometimes, 'If only we'd known!'

The stages of child development

0–6 months:	**Can I trust these people?**
6–18 months:	**Explore!**
18 months – 3 years:	**Learning to think.**
3–6 years:	**Other people.**
6–12:	**I did it my way!**
12–18 years:	**Getting ready to leave.**

Let's look at them in more detail.

The human baby arrives like a being from another planet. Its first thoughts and feelings are pretty blurry, but they are very much to do with:

'Am I safe?'

'Who's gonna feed me?'

'What happened to my waterbed?'

'Those people look nice. How can I keep them around?'

'What's that yukky feeling I'm sitting in?'

It is no use making demands of the new baby, or criticising it, since it is still just 'taking it all in'. It needs you to guess its needs (to be changed, fed, cuddled, burped, carried around) since it has no way of telling you what it wants.

It's important that you don't ignore its cries for help, since it will learn to become passive and depressed if ignored for long. It's equally important to let it *start* to cry heartily for a moment or two, so that it learns that it can *do something* to get its needs met, that its cries will bring help. A child who is always fed *before* it says it's hungry may have trouble knowing what it wants later in life.

Can I trust these people? 0–6 months

Massaging and cuddling the baby, making noises to it, looking at its face and smiling, all make for a happier, brighter child who subsequently sleeps, feeds and learns more easily. Massage has been found to cure constipated babies with amazing speed! (Stand well clear!)

Notice how babies from many of the wiser cultures are carried around in slings and carrybags? One Balinese tradition is the first 'setting down to earth' of a new baby – it does not take place until the child is six months old. Before this it is never out of somebody's arms! We would find this rather unmanageable but it's worth some thought.

This is the time when, at no charge to you, the child begins to educate himself! He moves out into the big, beautiful world, tasting, grabbing, pushing, carrying, pulling, eating everything in sight.

You can save yourself enormous amounts of energy by creating a *safe, child-proof* zone in your house, so that you don't need to be always saying '*don't*'. Put the stereo up high somewhere, postpone the new wallpaper, and your child will be free to wander in peace (yours).

The exploring stage goes wrong

In the mid–1970s, I was a very inexperienced psychology graduate, who knew more about rats than about children.

I began work as a School Guidance Officer. My role, according to my superiors, was to take children who, teachers felt, were stupid. I was to administer quaint little tests and then tell the teachers how stupid these children were. This was supposed to be helpful.

I don't really blame my superiors for devising this role. Being responsible for the psychological well-being of 3000 children in nine schools was daunting, and the little tests gave one something concrete to do.

I decided to do something more helpful than just IQ tests. I recruited and trained mothers to coach kids who had fallen behind in reading. I gave talks to teachers about self-esteem. I listened patiently to harassed parents. One day, I went on a home visit to the mother of a boy who was acting up at school…The home was out in the country and looked rather run down.

I took off my tie before going in. I talked rather awkwardly with the boy's Mum: she looked very old and tired. On the worn, dusty lino in the kitchen where we talked, a toddler sat looking dully up at us. There was not a Lego block or Dinky Toy in sight. From time to time the child tugged open a cupboard and pulled at the utensils inside. The mother would stand up, rebuke the child, slam the cupboard door and continue talking.

As I drove home, I felt very angry and helpless. That Mum's idea of a good toddler was a silent, still toddler. I knew that – without toys to play with and without encouragement to play, or look at books or hear stories – that child, too, would be on the Guidance Officer's list before many years had elapsed: 'suspected mentally deficient'.

Explore the world! 6–18 months

Children at this age need to be free of demands to perform, such as sitting up primly, being cute, or being toilet trained (the sphincter muscles that control your child's 'outlets' are not yet sufficiently developed for full control).

Physically, toddlers can be tiring, so this is a good age for you to start getting breaks of a few hours yourself, to rest and do your exploring!

Learning to think – 18 months–3 years

Now the child is starting to use reasoning. It's a good time to give simple explanations for things: 'The kitten gets scared when you squeeze her. I'll show you how to stroke her gently.'

Your child is also using anger and learning to say, 'No, I don't want to', 'I don't care'. This is the age called by some people 'The terrible twos'. Parents will need to set clear limits.

The child will test these. The parents must remain firm...and firm...and firm.

Work out ahead of time what is really important and what doesn't matter, to save energy. The child will sometimes want to be independent and then switch back to being very dependent again, especially if a new infant arrives on the scene. This is natural, and the child will soon 'grow up' again if its needs are met.

This is the age when children clearly move from playing alongside other children to playing *with* other children. It helps if there are other children to learn with. It's also the time of endless questions: when? why? how? what if? why not? and why again?

When they're chattering your ears off think of this as language development time, and count the money you're saving in remedial tuition and expensive school fees later in life!

Other people 3–6 years

Teasing or ridicule by parents, never a good idea, are particularly unhelpful at this age, when the child is learning how to be one of the human race and may easily withdraw.

Fantasy and reality need to be clearly separated: both are okay, but you need to know the difference.

'I'm a monster!'
'You're good at *pretending* to be a monster!'
Growl! Giggle!

Clear requests for appropriate behaviour can be made and are best phrased specifically and positively: 'Pick up your cars now' rather than 'Don't be untidy'.

Vera is the sort of parent that makes you feel like being a kid. Are you imagining it, or does she actually smell of home-made scones? She's also quick minded and humorous, and able to put a young psychologist in his place. I decide it's better in this workshop to learn from her than try to teach her, and sure enough I do. Vera recounts how her eight-year-old, Dale, had developed, ever so gradually, a temper that had become a problem to him and to other people. After one particular blow-up of Dale's, Vera had given the matter some careful thought, and then set about a profound and original cure.

She took down an old dusty album of family photos (never before seen by the children) and she and Dale looked through them. Vera pointed out the various family patriarchs, Grandfather Les when he was a boy, Great Uncle Alf, cousin Derek, where they had lived and what they had done. Dale looked with fascination at the weathered faces and ancient clothing styles, while Vera provided the narrative 'Alf was a good bloke, but very stubborn. Grandfather had quite a temper when he was a boy, so they say'. There was a pause as Dale wondered where this was leading. Vera just turned the pages. 'What happened with his temper, Mum?' 'Oh he just grew out of it I suppose. Look, here's his cricket team…'

Soon the other children came in, and Vera left them with the photos, and went to get the tea. Dale, of course, though he could be firm at times, never lost his temper again. He just grew out of it, I suppose.

I did it my way! 6–12 years

What makes it possible for a six to twelve-year-old to navigate the world of school, friends, and life generally, is his or her knowledge of the way things work and the 'rules of life'. These rules can be anything from 'If I share my toys with her she'll be my friend' to 'If I don't take my raincoat I'll get wet, and might get a cold and miss out on going ice skating'.

Parents will help by being firm on those rules that are important, but negotiating and compromising on those that are negotiable. The child thus learns the give-and-take skills that make up so much of adult life.

Challenging and arguing with the child, especially if you are not domineering but genuinely interested, will help the child refine her or his thinking abilities and better understand other people's needs. Self-care by parents is essential so that they can continue this challenging and hassling while maintaining warmth and good humour.

Parents also need to have their own interests and directions away from parenting, so that they are not tempted to dominate or be over-involved with their child's world, or to use their child in place of adult company. This is particularly important for single parents.

Getting ready to leave 12–18 years

Hard as it may seem (or perhaps you're glad?) this is the age of moving away from family, and moving in again, and away again, practising for the real jump into adult life. Although the child does not yet actually leave, his interests and energies are increasingly outside the family.

Some parents feel resentful that this is just a taxi-driving stage – which reflects more on our public transport systems (or lack thereof) and the dangers of our streets at night than anything else. Taxi-ing at least provides a good opportunity to talk.

Three important things are happening:

- The teenager moves forward like the tide – in waves, in and out. One minute he is independent, another wanting to be fed and nursed. One minute he is impressively reasonable, another rebellious and argumentative. Knowing that this will happen makes it easier to handle. Despite the waves, the tide is making progress.
- Sexuality is blossoming. A young person needs to hear that sex is good, that sexuality is welcome and healthy, and that it carries some decision-making responsibilities. Parents will not

act seductively, or respond to seductiveness from the young person, except to say, 'Someone is going to be delighted with you!'

- The break is going to come. Some young adults move out easily and slowly, but most don't! You can recognise that the young person may need to create and maintain disagreement in order to create the energy to break loose. Don't take this too personally. Like giving birth, releasing young adults is a little painful but well worth the trouble.

KIDS AND TV – THE GREAT DEBATE

Most kids see a lot of TV. In fact the average child now spends much more time in front of TV than they spend in classrooms at school! Not just the time spent, but also what is watched is a concern. Studies have pointed out that a child by their mid-teens will have seen tens of thousands of violent incidents, and thousands of deaths, portrayed in cartoon and realistic form – and this is only in children's viewing hours.

The exposure to violence and cheap life values is the most frequent concern about TV watching by kids. The next is what it stops kids from doing – it takes time up which they would normally spend running, jumping, playing, talking, reading and being creative – if they weren't beguiled by the hypnotic flow of the TV screen.

If you're a parent, I ask you to try just one thing – to watch your kids as they watch TV. You may find it a little chilling to see the slightly open mouthed, blank-eyed stare which kids develop after a time. They are clearly in an 'altered state' – never, in any area of life will you see children so passive and absorbent. By comparison, when reading books, their minds work vigorously as they imagine what the words conjure up. Driving in the car, playing in the yard, going to a circus, they are animated and interactive, 'chewing up' the world with their minds. But in front of a TV they soon drift into that old stare again, the active part of their brain is 'out to lunch'. Have a look yourself, and judge whether you like what you see.

Young children are particularly affected by what they see on the screen. We once had a four-year-old staying at our house, and he came out for a cuddle before bedtime. We were watching a comedy show, and a sketch came on in which an E. T. type creature's hand came out of a cupboard, rejected some chips and some lollies, but grabbed the child and pulled it in – then burped! It was subtly done, with no real drama – just wry adult humour. I glanced at the child's face though just to check, and noticed his jaw very set. 'Are you okay Ben?'

'Go away!'

'What are you angry about?'

'That boy got eaten!'

with which he started to cry, and we spent a good five minutes comforting him and trying to make light of the incident. We were moved by Ben's compassion and a little ashamed that we'd exposed him to unnecessary pain. We wondered if a life of nightmares would ensue! Older kids though, will watch horrific scenes without apparent reaction. Are they desensitised? Is that a good thing or a bad thing? No-one really knows.

Guidelines

If you are a little alarmed and want to do something about what your children watch, here are some suggestions for assessing kids' TV...

Language – not just swearing – but the quality and richness of verbal skills. Here's a simple test: listen to your child's programme for a minute or two without the picture (or go around the corner and listen to the dialogue). Is that the kind of talking you want your child to learn? Aaargh! Urghh! Take that! I'll teach you to...

Imagination – some kids only know how to play very restricted games – shooting, screaming, hitting. Perhaps this is a symptom that this is all they are watching on TV. It's possible to select kids' TV with a much wider range of themes. A special set of videos called *Kaboodle* was produced in Australia to improve what kids saw on TV, using many different styles of live and animated programmes. Kids we know think they're great, so good in fact that they pass the best test of kids' fare – you can stand to watch them yourself! Some movies and programmes for kids are simply stunning in imagination, depth and challenge.

Values – this means the hidden message in the film – which has a powerful effect on kids because it is largely unconscious. Common values problems include:

- Bad guys and good guys – some people are villains. They have deep voices and look funny. They are all bad. It's okay to kill them. Some people are all good. They are handsome and bland.

- Conflict is always a result of the bad guys being mean, until the good guys get revenge. It's okay to hurt the bad guys for what they've done. Revenge is sweet. There is no negotiation or middle ground. There are no reasons or sides to the conflict. Action – the more violent the better – is the answer to conflict.
- Sex roles – this is one that really should have gone away by now. But still in programmes from *Dr Who* to *Ninja Turtles*, the girls are cute, beautiful, have high pitched voices, and need rescuing. Boys or men are weapons- and action-oriented, always flying the spaceship, making the decisions, rescuing the girls. And they don't cry – ever!

Advertising – are the shows produced by toy companies to be in effect a half-hour ad for toy figures or accessories? Are the ads all for junk food or overpriced fad toys? Wouldn't it be cheaper if your TV got stuck on the BBC?

News – don't mistake the news for education. It is actually a form of entertainment – and often gives a distorted and unrealistic view of the real world. It's not suitable for primary aged children, and we don't think in its present form it does much for adults either. Watching the news can make you paranoid and depressed – and ill-informed about the world we live in.

What about educational TV?

Some children's TV is magnificent. Since the 1960s there have been concerted efforts made to use the potential of TV to help especially disadvantaged kids get a 'head start' with all the basic skills they will need as they enter school, and help them compete with kids from richer and more stimulating backgrounds. *Sesame Street* has taken a legendary role in this – and is still unmatched for the degree of thought and depth that goes into its content. (Though it has been criticised for being too 'fast' in attempting to hold kids' attention.)

Research has found that *Sesame Street* and similar programmes work much better if parents watch alongside their children, from time to time, and sing the songs or comment on the characters, and help their kids 'participate' with the programme – in this way avoiding the glazed-eye syndrome once again. The makers of the programme realised this need long ago, and deliberately lace the programme with subtler humour and ironies to interest adult viewers. They also have rock stars and other celebrities as guests to deliberately ensure that parents will turn the show on and occasionally watch it with their kids.

In Summary

There are lots of bright spots in kids' TV. *Playdays* has remained enormously popular for toddlers because the presenters don't talk down to the kids, but TO them, in such a way that kids will often hold conversations with the TV!

Many parents now restrict what their kids watch in quantity and quality. They allocate an hour, or two hours, per day, and negotiate which programmes. This encourages children to plan, be selective, and savour 'their' programme rather than just watching an endless stream. Put the TV in a room away from your living area so that it doesn't dominate family life.

It's probably a good idea not to get so uptight about children's TV that it becomes a huge conflict. But considering that it's the biggest influence on their minds after you, you may want to monitor your kid's TV diet.

HOW TO STOP WHINGEING KIDS

Have you noticed how some adults have really pleasant voices? And that some children also have melodious, clear tones that are a pleasure to listen to? And have you also noticed that there is nothing harder on your ears than a kid who is always whingeing and whining. Talking through her nose?! AAAAWWWWWW Muhhhhhhhmmmmmmm?

Did you know that the tone of voice we use – as adults or kids – is simply a habit? Not just a habit of voice, but also of attitude to life! Whining comes from the 'helpless' part of us that wants others to fix it all up, that is never satisfied, that grizzles and complains. Whenever we talk with a whine, we will feel this way too. Whingeing kids, if uninterrupted, will grow into whingeing adults. (Behind every nagging husband or moaning wife is a parent who gave in to a whinger). But whingeing and whining can be stopped overnight! Here's how...

First you have to understand how the pattern starts, it's simple enough. A child asks us for something, first of all quietly, then loudly. We say no, or else ignore them. They then move into phase two – they rev up into full-scale whining. It's probably accidental at first – they just discover by chance a tone of voice that we just can't ignore! We will often give in to them, just for some peace and quiet. If the pattern repeats often enough, they learn to depend on it, and before you know it – you have a whingeing kid.

So what do you do?

1) Tell 'em. Next time they start whingeing at you, make direct eye contact. Then ask them straight out – 'use a normal voice please.'
2) Teach 'em how. Find out if they actually know how to speak in a lower sounding voice – firm, but deeper in note. Try them out until they get it right. Demonstrate for them so they can hear what you mean.
3) Make it stick. Start the campaign. Whenever they whinge at you for something, say to them 'Use a normal voice'. The choice of words is important – you are getting them to realise that whining is not normal – for them, or anyone else. Make sure that they get what they are asking for only by asking more positively.

Of course even if they get to sound like the Queen's New Year speech, don't give in to them if it doesn't suit you – they still have to learn to take no for an answer. Once again, be realistic, they are learning the way of the world – that people will like you better and respond more positively if you sound pleasant and strong, rather than helpless and negative.

8

Energy and how to save it

Good news – your children need you healthy and happy.

I once lived for a month in a coastal village of Papua New Guinea. Children there did not live with their own parents but moved about in small groups, staying first in one house and then in another. Seven-year-olds could be seen carrying babies or tending cooking fires. By fourteen they were doing adult work with confidence and pride. As the newest and most interesting thing in the village, I had a dozen or so kids sleeping at my 'house', but I presumed that if I became boring enough they would go elsewhere. When tropical diarrhoea struck in the small hours of the night, I had to pick my way out through a carpet of small brown bodies.

It occurred to me that this would be an easy place to be a parent since the work and pleasure of parenting was shared by the whole village. In fact, any adult who was present *was* a parent.

In our society, parenting is not shared, and it's not safe for small children to move about the community.

It's easy to feel, then, that you have to become 'Superparent' and somehow meet by yourself all the needs of your kids for entertainment, education, love and affection, food, drink, safety, clothing and cleaning. If you're the parent who stays at home with the kids, you feel over-domesticated and housebound and yearn for adult company. If you're the parent who goes out making the money, you feel like a workhorse, with too little home and family in your life. It's little wonder that many parents, especially the parents of two or more children under five, are almost permanently exhausted, irritable and in borderline health.

When we feel well, and in good company, and healthy and rested, we can give to our children and enjoy doing it. When we feel tired, sick, lonely and overburdened, there is a point at which kids become a threat, a competitor in the struggle for survival. This point can easily be dangerous, to you, your marriage and the safety of your kids.

Overstretched parents eventually reach a point at which they can parent no longer. It is vital that you learn to take care of yourself: only then can you parent well. Your kids need you happy and healthy. This brief chapter will tell you how to be and stay that way.

I often talk with parents who don't understand why they aren't coping. They expect superhuman performance without realising that human beings need 'fuel'. They don't just run on food: they need 'energy' in the form of love, recognition, touch and talking with others.

Every person you talk to or meet either takes energy away from you or gives you energy. That's why we speak of some people as being 'draining'. It's also the reason we dread certain people ringing us up, or drive 100 kilometres just to see a special friend for an hour or two.

Kids can give energy back to us, but for the most part it is right and proper that we recharge them. However, when we are their only source of refuelling and we dry up on them, something is bound to happen.

Think for a moment. Where is your energy tank right now, as you are reading this book?

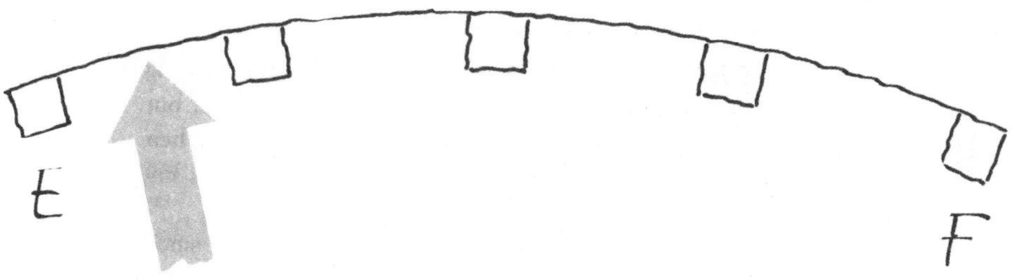

Is this where you usually keep it? Are you always (as in the song) 'Running on empty'?

We often treat our bodies as we treat our cars: five dollars' worth at a time, bald tyres and long overdue for a tune-up!

You might like to look at the people in your life and consider how they help or hinder your fuel reserves. Sometimes people realise that their 'friends' are simply 'stealing' energy and giving nothing back. Time to find some new friends! People who were once good for us (including parents!) may now be a source of only negative feelings. You can, if you wish, change the way you interact with people so that you move to positive exchanges instead.

Hello, dear, I've had a dreadful week!

I've had a good one. Let me tell you about it.

God, there were so many problems at the office today.

Well, I could listen while you tell me about them. Or would you prefer to plan our next holiday?

It's a neat strategy and, carried out with good humour, benefits both parties.

With a group of twenty young parents, I once spent a couple of hours listing the ways that parents can 'refuel their tanks'. We came up with quite a few good ideas.

- Get a babysitter.
- Learn to be boring to your children so they leave you in peace for a while.
- Spend 10 minutes with your partner when he or she comes home from work: exchange *good news* or just be together. (If the kids can sit quietly, they can be there; if not, send them into another room.)
- Spend half an hour of *full-attention* time with children each day, instead of hours of begrudged half-attention. Let children plan and look forward to what they want to do with you in *their* half-hour.
- Learn to *switch off* in a comfortable way, so that you relax and think nice thoughts as you do housework, commute to work, or whatever.
- Cook food sometimes the way *you* like it instead of always eating kids' food.
- Play *your* music.
- Spend plenty of time with other parents.
- Be clear about what you are asking of your partner: affection, sex or just company. Try to meet and understand each other's needs as they arise. If you usually just talk when you're tense, try massage. If you usually just touch, try talking.
- On a regular basis, do one activity that is not concerned with being a parent but is an *adult-satisfying activity*, just for you. Whether this is with other people or alone is up to you.

When some new-born babies 'meet' their mothers, they do not bond well, and changing and feeding are a struggle in which baby and mother are tense and unhappy. One hospital introduced a program for rebonding which is beautiful in its simplicity, and symbolic of the whole parenting process. The staff realised that mother and baby were caught in a vicious circle. They solved this by sitting the mother on a bean bag and the father behind on a chair. The father gently massaged the mother's shoulders and back, enabling her to relax. The mother held and stroked the infant, perhaps feeding it, too. If the mother was a single parent, then a male member of staff would massage the mother instead; and if the father felt tense or awkward, then a physiotherapist might even stand behind him and massage his shoulders.

The unique nature of touch, giving both energy and reassurance, enables humans to soften and move out of tense patterns. It is so often forgotten…but it beats tranquillisers every time!

- Use all the kinds of support and help around: neighbourhood houses, child health centres, fitness clubs (especially the friendly, non-commercial kind), sports, playgroups and creches, parent effectiveness classes.
- Use a creche or baby-sitting co-operative for '*self-time*', instead of only for rushing around the shops or to a job.
- Learn that 'Messy Is Beautiful' and give up 'tidy house' ideals for a few years. (You can always leave a vacuum cleaner by the door and say to visitors, 'Gee, I was just about to start cleaning up!')
- Have kids' areas of the house, where valuable things are not around and surfaces and furniture are easy to clean. This saves the wasted energy of a thousand 'Don'ts' a day.
- Have tidy and beautiful areas of the house (even if it's only your bedroom) where kids aren't allowed to go – so that you have somewhere nice to be.

- Talk, solve problems, figure out plans in the lounge room, sitting down, face to face, with the kids out of the way. Don't make bed the family parliament. Bed is for better purposes than that.

There are a lot of bad rumours around about parenting – things like: with young children you have no time for yourself; you'll have to wait until they're older before you can relax; your partner will have to be patient, the kids need you most. None of these are true. Parenting is meant to be fun.

But I don't have time for me!

The parents who really suffer are those who set very high standards and put their own needs far down the list. 'But doctor, I don't understand it. I had just finished redecorating the spare room and baking the three-tiered cake for Damian's party when this awful headache started. Could you give me something for it because I have to hurry back and finish making Darlene's disco dress?'

In fact, there are three simple responsibilities you have as a parent. Here they are, *in order of importance*:

- take care of yourself;
- take care of your partnership;
- take care of your kids.

People used to think that, to be a parent, you had to make huge sacrifices and become a doormat. Small wonder that so many people today are opting to have no kids at all. Those same people who saw parenting as a self-denying task can be heard in middle and older life saying things like, 'After all I did for you' and 'We gave you the best years of our life', trying to recapture with guilt the debt they feel they've incurred. The fact is that parenting is something you do for yourself.

It follows, then, that caring for you, your partnership and your kids actually go hand in hand. Looking after yourself makes you happier and more giving – you're giving out of choice, and from a position of fulfilment.

Looking after your partnership reminds you you're a valued and attractive adult, not just a childminder or a breadwinner in the other person's eyes. You have a sense of stability that enables you to relax, but you have enough growth and change taking place to enable you to remain interested in and excited by your partner.

Looking after your kids flows naturally from the above: if you feel that you have chosen parenting as one of your goals, if you are self-caring and have partnerships and friendships that sustain you and remind you of your worth, then giving to children will come easily. Your tank will often be full and your children won't need to start panic buying! End of sermon.

Saving energy with the 'soft no'

Jerrem is two-and-a-half, and a handful. He seems to have learned infant-assertiveness, and makes demands over and over until something happens – whether it's to have ice-cream for tea, to interrupt Mum on the phone, or to get that shiny toy at the supermarket checkout.

His mother, Allie, is luckily discovering how to deal with all of this. Firstly she knows that this is a normal developmental stage for children of Jerrem's age, and that it won't last for ever. Secondly, she has just mastered the 'soft-no' technique, and has become invincible!

She sees other mothers struggle with their two-year-olds, and sees them caught up in rising tension:

I wannit! No
I WANNIT! NO!
I WANNIT I WANNIT I WANNIT!
NO YOU CAN'T HAVE IT!

The mothers become angry and tense and upset with themselves, assuming that they must match their infants' red-faced loudness in order to win.

Allie, however, does it differently. She simply says no, quite softly (knowing that children have excellent hearing). If Jerrem persists, she says it again, equally softly, at the same time relaxing her shoulders and softening her whole body (a trick which took a few hours to master). If Jerrem shouts, especially in a public place, she imagines herself carrying him bodily to the car, but at the same time softens and smiles inwardly. She controls her own feelings, rather than letting little Jerrem control them. The temptation to yell at him occasionally returns, but imagining the way he would enjoy this victory, soon removes this temptation.

Allie is puzzled that just as she mastered the 'soft-no' skill, Jerrem seems to have stopped his hassling.

FOOD AND KIDS' BEHAVIOUR

Would you change your kids' diet, if you knew it would make them do really well at school, be calm and happy in themselves, and twice as pleasant to be around? Of course you would. Did you know that poor food intake is thought by some to be the major factor in juvenile crime? And did you know that the same changes to diet can help you feel better, have more energy, and perhaps avoid being overweight without eating any less?

Sometimes it's important to go back to the basics – and there's nothing much more basic than food. We're discovering that what people feed to their children, and when, has a profound effect on them.

Here are some simple guidelines on the psychological effects of food:

1) Choose food that gives steady energy. Food serves two purposes. It provides nutrients for growing and for repairing our bodies; and it also gives us energy for physical and mental activity. Most people these days provide their kids with a range of foods to give a nourishing diet. But it's also important to give the right kind of energising food – complex carbohydrates, and protein foods, which give a steady, day-long release of energy into a child's system. This kind of diet will prevent fatigue, promote a steady, focused state of mind, and help children to feel settled and easy. In particular, children need to eat complex carbohydrates – wholegrain food, high protein food, and perhaps some fresh food such as fruit, for breakfast each day.
2) Eat it before you need it. That's right – breakfast! Breakfast is the meal which will provide energy through the day. Eating substantial foods in the afternoon or evening may nourish you and your kids, but the energy input will be wasted. Eating your main food intake just before you become active will also avoid obesity – food goes straight into the bloodstream where it's needed. But when children or adults eat a big meal in the evening, and then sit about or sleep, the food, instead, is laid down into their fatty reserves. People can eat just as much, but by changing when they eat it, they'll find that this will reduce weight problems.

   We suggest that you experiment. Give your children protein food such as eggs, egg-flips, meat, or fish with their breakfast each day for two weeks. (If they complain they aren't hungry at breakfast time, give them less for dinner the night before!) See for yourself how much more settled and happy they are at home and school.
3) Avoid 'quick burnout' foods. Sugar, and refined sugary foods have a markedly unpleasant effect on kids' behaviour. Many children have simply too much energy minutes after eating such rapid release foods. They become edgy, hyperactive, and just plain naughty. Blood tests show that this energy release peaks quickly, and the child's blood sugar drops below where it started, as the

body struggles to cope. Thus children have a mid-morning sag, where they cannot concentrate, and act lazy and unfocused.

4) Avoid chemicals, dyes and preservatives. Additives and dyes in food have complex and individual effects. When I visit kindergartens these days I often see charts reminding teachers which child is allergic to what. They almost need a computer to keep track. It seems wrong that the human body is so reactive to natural foods – perhaps additives and residues have made some kids hypersensitive to what was previously safe to eat.

As well as observing what *your* child reacts to, some foods are generally a problem for almost every child. The need to reduce sugar has already been mentioned especially at breakfast and lunchtime. Tartrazine (E102) which is found in yellow-dyed foods can cause violent bouts of hyperactivity in children. Phosphates (found in processed foods such as hot dogs, commercial hamburgers, processed cheese, instant soup and toppings) are also strongly implicated.

The simplest and most effective thing you can do is feed your kids more of the complex or protein foods earlier in the day – they just won't get as hungry for junk. Likewise, if your child is going to a party where the parents are still living in the 1950s diet wise (soft drinks, cakes, ice-cream and lollies!), then feed your kids up with good stuff before they go – and minimise the damage!

Don't get too uptight about food all at once, because it is an emotional subject for kids too. Just start a steady, gradual, but determined programme.

Convincing studies support this common sense approach to nutrition – in the September 1988 edition, *New Internationalist* reported a study involving 3000 young offenders, who experienced 70–80 percent reductions in criminal behaviour over twelve months while on a high nutrition diet.

We will need a lot fewer psychologists, psychiatrists, and even police officers, when people once again have a good breakfast!

9

Special situations

How you can help if you're a teacher, a politician, a grandparent, neighbour or friend.

How you can help if you're a primary school teacher, a secondary school teacher, a politician or community activist, a grandparent, neighbour or friend).

By the time a child gets to playgroup you will be able to recognise 'negative programming' very clearly.

Here are the main indicators:

If you're a primary school teacher: how to counteract negative programming in the children you teach

- a child who hangs back from other children, looks sad or agitated and does not respond to overtures of friendship from other children;
- a child who joins in but, when presented with a learning task or activity, will not try it and looks fearful or distracted if approached on a one-to-one basis;
- a child who hits out at other children and reacts inappropriately when spoken to (for example, by laughing when chastised) and does not seem to have positive exchanges with other children.

You may have children in your class who fall into one of these three categories, or you may find children with a combination of the three.

For the sake of simplicity, let's look at them one at a time.

The sad and lonely child

It is most useful to regard this kind of child as having missed out on affection and on being valued and affirmed in the early part of life (0–2 years). He needs positive messages that are not tied to performance but are simply strokes for 'being', such as 'Hello Eric, nice to see you'. A friendly touch or hug with the child, being careful not to make her seem different from the others, also provides reassurance.

Such strategies, spread out over some days and weeks, should result in the child visibly relaxing and loosening up in the class-room and then beginning to initiate contacts with you – showing you work, smiling at you as you scan the room, speaking to you, and so on.

The self-critical child who won't give things a try

This child may have had its needs met in the early part of life but has been subjected to verbal put-downs consistently since he was old enough to listen (which was, of course, very young). The pattern tends to occur a lot where a loving mother has a second baby and shifts to being verbally critical of the first child.

Many parents, especially when they themselves are having a tough time, will put the children down as a matter of course, almost every time they speak to them. The children from such situations (probably at least one in ten children) will actually say things like 'I'm stupid', 'I can't' or 'I'm a dumb-dumb' if asked why they won't attempt some new task.

The remedy will be obvious to you: give positive affirmations very consistently to these children. Ideally, give positive messages both for performance and for just being. For example, 'You did that really well', 'I like your ideas for paintings', 'It's nice to see you this morning!' or just plain 'Hello'. Don't gush though – make quiet, understated comments which they can tolerate.

You will have to make sure that you avoid using put-downs with the child (who may actually invite them) and that you use assertive statements rather than 'you' statements to control the child.

For example, use 'Go and get your bag now!' instead of 'You're so forgetful, Anna!'

For really lasting impact, though, the child's parents will need some help, too. You will probably find, if they come to the school, that they are tired, overworked and possibly resentful and defensive. Your best approach would be a casual and friendly chat before broaching the problem, rather than a 'Your kid is a problem' full-frontal attack!

You can simply explain that you have noticed their child's self-esteem is low and ask if they find they easily criticise him or call him names. Explain that you, too, feel this way when you're tired but you've realised how children can take it to heart to a surprising degree.

Parents of kids in this category will be the ones most helped by reading this book. You could lend them a copy!

The child who is aggressive towards other kids and sarcastic to you

I saved this one till last! This child can be best understood as having been fully hooked on a 'negative' culture, being both handled in an aggressive way and shown by example only negative ways of relating. It is very likely that the child's parents fight routinely, in words if not in actions.

Significantly, the child is not *choosing* to interact using aggression – it may be the only way he knows *how* to interact.

It is very important to realise that, initially, this kind of child will not often respond to warmth and praise (but it's worth a try).

The teacher must first of all establish a bond through the mode the child can hear – that of firm controlling, and often negative interactions. This can be done, of course, without using put-downs.

Thus, in the early weeks, a firm hand on the shoulder (not pinching or controlling, though) and a clear request for behaviour ('stop doing that now, and come over here to get a book', 'Sit down now and start your drawing') are the necessary reactions from you.

The way to establish a beneficial and significant relationship with an aggressive child is to persist – firmly and without becoming angry or irritated. Eye contact, especially with humour behind the eyes as you reinforce your firmness, will signal that you are powerful enough to contain the child, so that he or she can begin to relax.

Once this relationship has been established, the positive messages can be added for doing positive things. This differs from what the parents may have done – only noticing the child when he played up.

These children are often the most responsive to having special roles (such as 'equipment collector') – roles with a genuine responsibility and privilege As they develop a 'friendship' with you, that is, the skill of exchanging positive messages – they will be able to extend this to other children.

Negatively programmed children are very much in evidence in secondary schools. In fact, the nature of secondary school can easily worsen the programming. If you want to help these children, or even if you just would like to know how to handle problem kids better for your own peace of mind, read on!

You may have heard of Ivan Illich, a educator who has something unkind to say about nearly all the institutions of the western world! Luckily, he does this with some creativity, and occasionally suggests a solution! Illich says that the real reason we have schools is to prepare people for life in factories (or, if they are really well behaved, office blocks). This, he argues, is why our schools are so factory-like – young people can get used to being a nobody, doing what they're told and producing things.

If you're a secondary school teacher

It's not really that bad…is it? However, secondary schools do suffer from some dehumanising aspects in their basic design. In particular, huge numbers (often over 1000 in a school, although research suggests that 200–300 is the ideal size); no home base (students are never on their own territory and often even change groupings so that they do not stay with the same friends); and impersonal teaching (learning from so many different teachers, who teach so many classes that they would be heard pressed even to know your name, not to mention know you personally enough to care about you in any but the most generalised way).

In my research I have found that students have four major problems with secondary school: the work; sarcasm and put-downs from teachers; loneliness; put-downs and aggression from other kids. It is appropriate for us to address here the last three of these problems.

As a child, I attended a bay-side high school near Melbourne. It had a combination (which I later realised was not uncommon) of a gentle, but somewhat ineffectual, principal and a vice-principal who was a thug.

On one occasion I saw a boy thrown out of the vice-principal's door and land backwards against lockers on the opposite wall, without touching the ground on the way. The vice-principal had personality traits which would lead me, unhesitatingly (now that I am trained in the field), to seek to have him locked up!

I would stress that I do not blame the individual person as much as the collusion of other staff and of an education department that not only employs but also promotes such people. Hopefully, things have improved since those days.

Another experience that coloured my experience of secondary school was the fate of a close friend who far outstripped the other students academically. Gaining high marks in the final year and securing scholarships to university, he was nonetheless dissatisfied with his own exam performance, bought a rifle and took his own life.

Four children committed suicide at that school while I was a student there and the school swimming hero is currently in prison after an unsuccessful fight with drug addiction. I consider all to have been victims, and their fates to have been easily preventable. When people ask me where my energy for humanising education comes from, this is one of the a dozen stories I can choose by way of explanation.

Sarcasm and put-downs from teaching staff

This is a symptom of unhappiness and frustration in the teacher. Few non-teachers have any idea of the stress and difficulty of teaching in secondary schools in the nineties. Teachers come a close second to psychiatrists in the rate of work-caused physical and mental breakdowns.

A large, faceless school isn't any happier for the teacher than for the kids. Secondary schools, fuelled by the breakdown of families and the rise of epidemic unemployment and its hardships, are often physically menacing, emotionally harrowing places unless very concerted and innovative efforts are being made to humanise the school environment.

Sarcasm and aggressive attacks on children are used for two reasons. One is that they simply relieve the teacher's inner pressures: if the teacher was a happier person they would not take place. The second is that control of kids is a constant preoccupation and sarcasm works in getting kids to behave, at least in the short term.

One last plea. We all lose our temper and sound off from time to time. Kids can handle this. It's constant carping that hurts. If you don't basically like and enjoy kids, please don't be a teacher.

Isolation is also epidemic in secondary schools. Watch the school ground or corridor closely during a break. Some students will be visibly alone while another, larger group will be attached to cliques and grouping of student, but only loosely so, tagging along but rarely interacting with the others.

Boys will be more tolerant of appendages to their groups: girls tend to include or exclude more decisively. For this reason, you will also see pairs or trios of girls who stay together simply out of mutual loneliness, sometimes barely even talking.

Loneliness

In the classroom you will notice that some children lack even the most basic conversational skills. They will only be able to manage a mumbled word or two if spoken to and would never initiate a conversation unaided. Only recently are some English and speech and drama teachers beginning to tackle these vital skills.

Lonely kids tend to go unnoticed; their more noisy and aggressive counterparts are actually better off since they at least get some of the attention they are seeking. It may take a second look at the classes you teach to spot the loners and wordless ones, but they will certainly be there.

If you are willing to 'prioritise' the one or two lonely children in each class, deliberately making contact with them and showing an interest in their work, without drawing down on them the spotlight of class attention, then even this small amount of attention will not be wasted in the arid social life they lead.

Any efforts to humanise the school experience such as home rooms and home groups, excursions, camps, and deliberate teaching in the areas of social skills, relationships and self-esteem – will be of immense benefit. Secondary school is for many children the last chance to climb out of a negative program for life. Do what you can!

The legendary cruelty of kids to other kids is usually handled in a counter-productive way. The problem is, in fact, always a symptom of the adult system in which the children live. An oppressive overall system, at home or school, leads to the 'victims' taking it out on each other.

Peer aggression, in action and words

From time immemorial, when the barons were tough on the knights, the knights took it out on the peasants, and the peasants, instead of revolting (they lacked the resources for that), generally brutalised each other for light relief! When this dynamic is not understood, school authorities try to stop the persecution by persecuting and the overall result is greater tension and violence in the system.

Where teachers are given proper facilities and support in their jobs, and children are treated with firmness but allowed to keep their self-respect, then bullying of kids by kids rapidly dies away. Although material conditions in a school are important, they in no way compare with *how people treat each other*, from the top down.

School is not usually the source of children's more serious problems. Nonetheless, it does have a way of compounding the misery!

In a revealing study carried out for the Council of Adult Education in Melbourne, it was found that illiterate adults had almost universally suffered problems of adjustment before they even entered school. The school, however, failed to remedy the fearfulness and low self-esteem of these children, which became a handicap in their learning to read and write. (One-tenth of Australian adults have significant literacy problems.)

The failure of schools to help problem children is in no way the fault of the classroom teacher. The fault lies in the whole method of 'factory-schooling': we attempt to teach children in herds of 30 to 40 at a time, and wonder that so many do not learn well. We are the only culture in history that has taken such an approach to educating our young; thousands of years ago Aborigines were teaching young people on a one-to-one basis and had no failures or dropouts.

In summary

No teacher, however dedicated, can be both the emotional support and learning stimulus that 30 children need in order to learn well. Soon the day will come when we reassess education and learn to flood our schools with skilled adults, volunteer and paid, trained and training so that each child gets his due. Until then, education will be an uphill battle, with many casualties.

Since you are a caring teacher (or you would not be reading this) and since you want to do as much as you can *now*, let me conclude by urging you to:

eliminate put-downs from your classroom and use assertive methods of control;
when faced with problem children, who may already be taking much of your time and nervous energy, consider using the methods outlined in this chapter;
be sure to meet your *own* needs for positive strokes and affirmation. You are an endangered species and your children need you healthy and alive!

If you're a politician or community activist!

A family is not an island. Healthy families can only exist in a society that supports their needs. Society can be seen as a kind of gigantic social club, to which we all pay membership fees, help to fundraise and do the work for, and in return receive various benefits.

The social club is far from perfect. Not only is it rather disorganised, but members with vested interests different from our own work constantly to change its direction in their favour. We thus have to work hard to make sure that we and others get our part of the bargain, while at the same time being co-operative enough so that the club does not collapse.

Parents in particular find that they need to keep dealing with the world to get a fair deal for their children. Thus, as well as directing energies 'inwards' to improve family life by playing with and educating children, and spending time with one's partner, parents may find themselves focusing 'outwards' to society, being on school committees, neighbourhood organisations, right through to a strong political commitment or religious or other causes.

Naturally people can overbalance in either direction. On one extreme we find the uninvolved family that does not venture into community life, and can thus be herded like sheep into an increasingly totalitarian state. In contrast we find the parents who are so politically involved (or career involved, or cause-involved) that they have no family life and so become increasingly dehumanised.

This book has been an 'inwards' book , dealing with life within the family unit – a worthwhile focus but one needing balance. This brief section looks at how our new understanding of family life affects the wider picture.

The diagram on the following page shows what is sometimes called the 'social contract' – what we receive for our membership in society. The picture looks very 'one-way', but in reality this is not the case. The family gives its labour, taxes, and in many other ways contributes to society. In fact the family multiplied by millions IS society. The family, however, often finds that it is in some way being short-changed – perhaps health care is poor or too expensive, or it is cut off from social facilities, or jobs do not exist for the family's teenagers. This requires the family to fight for what it needs.

In dozens of parent workshops I have talked about 'parents rights', and found that parents are unsatisfied with services, such as schools, doctors, local government, and so on. Allowing for the natural tendency of humans to enjoy a good grumble, it's clear that many people feel powerless and short-changed by the society around them, and especially by 'the authorities'. The concepts of assertiveness apply here too, and we now teach parents through role-play and strategy-rehearsal to deal with vague doctors, rude public servants, arrogant teachers, and so on, and to get their rights in consumer dealings too.

Assertiveness in the wider arena must include organised action, since single voices only have limited power. More and more in the nineties, people are joining interest groups and movements. No longer do they opt for trivial time-filling groups (the tennis-court-improvement-cake-bake-auxiliary) nor do they favour larger faceless groups such as traditional political parties, but more mid-range movements such as environmental lobby groups, school involvement groups, and so on.

Politicians should welcome this tendency, since it is the road to real participatory democracy, as well as being a low cost solution to community development in otherwise isolated and anonymous modern cities. A caring, close neighbourhood does far more to prevent child abuse (through its removal of loneliness and boredom) that any number of doctors and social workers. Self-help groups such as MIND (for mental health), Parents Anonymous (for child protection), Alcoholics Anonymous, National Childbirth Trust, School Involvement, Parents Without Partners, Vietnam Veterans, are proliferating *ad infinitum*, and doing a remarkable job.

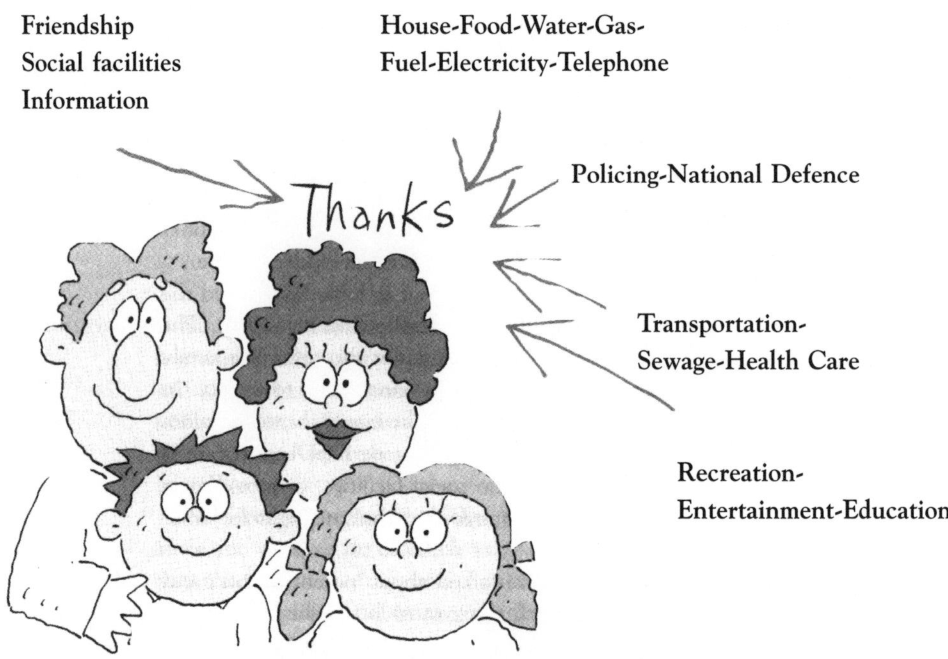

There is no doubt that families need material security first. Below a certain income level, no one can raise happy children. However, above a basic level the need changes. What people benefit from most once they are housed and fed adequately is a chance to be connected with others and involved in purposeful activity which has been freely chosen.

One often hears the complaint that parents 'don't want to get involved'. Usually this complaint comes from someone who conducts boring and alienating parent-teacher nights or preachy lectures on how to bring up children! Contrast this with the immense success of parties for looking at and buying plastic bowls and lacy underwear! Clearly people love to involve themselves in friendly, participatory gatherings, and will risk a surfeit of lunch boxes to do so! It's sad that such trivial gatherings are often the only way to meet the strong needs for communal belonging and interaction in our vast suburban homelands.

A large-scale statistical study in the US sought to find out why in spite of low income, broken homes, and poor housing, some teenagers remained law-abiding and productive, while others became criminal offenders. The only factor which emerged with any strength was that those who coped had access to adult involvement, outside their family, which was supportive and friendly. Most often, though not in all cases, this was through belonging to some club or group led by interested adults. Since incarceration of young offenders costs about $20,000 per person per year at the present time, youth work also seems a sound investment.

Let me sum up. If you are a parent, you will often need to get involved with groups and situations outside your own four walls, in order to advance your family's interests, and secure some kind of future for your children to live in. (It's interesting how much of the peace movement, for instance, is made up of young parents.) If you are involved in the community, whether as secretary of a mothers' club, or a parliamentarian, then the one thing you must understand is that families need to belong. Whatever helps to bond families together and build strong local communities will save money and trouble a hundredfold, and lead to a happier more self-reliant society in the future. When public money is being spent, prevention is definitely better than cure.

If you're a grandparent, neighbour or friend

Parenting can be a lonely business. Often it is only those people who live nearby or are close family who see the pressure building up and the negative put-down patterns beginning to develop between parent and child. It's difficult in this position, though, to know how to offer help in a way that won't offend. Let me make some suggestions.

Practical help The most obvious way you can help is babysitting. Many young parents are exhausted from the sheer endlessness of parenting and earning a living. A couple of hours' relief may be life-saving, and yet is something that parents hesitate to ask for, for fear of imposing on you. Here's a hint: offer to baby-sit 'sometimes' and do so, but occasionally say, 'No, I won't be able to this week'. This lets the parents know that you can say no – and also means you won't be taken for granted! A friend of mine, who is crafty to match her years, offers to baby-sit for some young parents next door only if they agree to use the time for relaxation. Manipulative but effective.

Material help comes next. Out society seems to be built on a pattern whereby we are poor when we are raising our children, and have an excess of money when our children are grown up. In earlier times people were individually poorer, but could *share* in the family's collective property. The loan of all the equipment needed for raising children (prams, etc.) or other forms of material support is much appreciated by today's young family.

Friendship

There is nothing like warm, good-humoured availability, and a willingness to listen, in a neighbour or friend. Parents accumulate tension and worries as they go along and, with a sympathetic listener, these will tend to pour off like water through a breached dam. If you have the time to listen and enquire, and if you don't rush in with remedies or comparisons, you will visibly notice the relaxation spread on the person's face as he or she talks.

Don't preach, teach, judge, compare, criticise, evaluate or generally act like Dorothy Dix. If you feel the patronising glow of 'older and wiser' coming over you, then close your mouth and smile a lot until the feeling passes. Advice can be a blow to the self-esteem of the person receiving it, especially if it wasn't sought in the first place. Even if it's 'good' advice, it will have the unpleasant side-effect of making the person feel small. Take my advice!

What not to do!

If you are the parent's parent, this is an even greater hazard. You will be tempted again and again to slip in some of the parenting you overlooked when they were twelve years old, just at the moment when they are floundering and hoping you hadn't noticed. If you do this often your offspring will have to pretend to be coping whenever you're around – an added burden for them.

Adults need friends, and they need positive messages.

Supplementary parents

Margaret Mead once said that little kids and grandparents get on so well because they have a common enemy! Kids do need other adults, as friends, confidantes, and to give approval and affection at those times when parents are just too overtaxed to respond well. Even the crabbiest grandparent has his value, if only to show that Mum and Dad really are quite nice people by contrast! I know of many people who only made it through their childhood because in an otherwise unbearable home life there was one older person nearby who provided a safe harbour.

When families are woven in with friends and neighbours, and when people of all generations have access to each other, then we won't need psychologists or departments of social welfare. We'll take care of ourselves.

More Secrets of Happy Children

Introduction

Dear Reader,

It's fourteen years since I wrote my first book on parenting. My life has been greatly affected by people's responses to *The Secret of Happy Children* over those years. Whenever Shaaron and I travel around the world, it is like meeting friends who already know us. The confidence that people put in us makes us both proud and anxious. What inspires us is the fact that people everywhere care SO much about their kids.

Parenthood is deep water. It can occasionally make you happier than anything else in your life, but you will also sometimes feel like your heart is being kicked around on the footpath! Don't let anyone tell you that it is simple.

Today there are dozens of parenting books on the shelves. So logical and cheerful! Full of breezy advice and long tidy lists of what to do. Four steps to confident kids! Who are they kidding?

On the other hand, something has to be done – since many parents are desperate for answers. So, where does this second book fit in? It is a deeper book than the first one. It is also more specific, since it is based on work with thousands more parents who have told us what works. The ideas of softlove and firmlove, which you'll learn about in this book, are powerful tools that can turn family life around. They address the real aims of parenthood – to produce young adults with warm hearts and lots of backbone.

There are also two big challenges for mothers and fathers embedded in this book:

- to give up violence and fear-based methods of discipline
- to really raise your own children, and not leave this job to others.

It's clear that raising kids sends you on an inner journey of self- discovery. This is certainly worthwhile. So – no quick answers in this book. Instead, some powerful ideas to help you find 'your own right way'.

Much love to your family from ours,

Steve Biddulph

PS The wombats have grown up and left home!

1

Making tomorrow's people

Imagine this. You are sitting on the front porch. In front of you are gardens and a leafy street – there is no sound but the singing of birds. You are old, but still tanned and fit, and wearing warm, soft clothes.

A sleek and almost silent vehicle rolls up. Its doors click open, and some young adults step out. They are your grown-up children!

They give you big hugs. They are full of energy, and happy to see you. They sit down and tell you their latest adventures, new achievements and news of their families. You bring out food and drinks, and talk over many things. Eventually, it's time for them to leave.

You go inside and put on a warm sweater.

For a long time you sit by the window, remembering back to when they were children. You feel very proud of how they have turned out, of what you have given the world.

Seeing your kids as a gift

If you were to believe the media, you'd think that kids are nothing but one big problem – a behaviour problem, a childcare problem, a health problem.

This is a terrible con, because the truth is … kids are a beautiful gift. Deep down we really know this, but sometimes we forget. The one in five couples who have fertility problems know what a gift children are. So do the parents whose children battle with illness or disability. When our children are endangered, we suddenly realize that they matter so much, and that other things matter so little.

There *are* real challenges in raising kids. In this book we'll tackle many of these. But you should start by reminding yourself what a fantastic thing to have in your life – the shaping of a new life, the launching of a wonderful human being into the future. You will give and receive. Your life will be greatly enriched by the love and adoration you can receive from your children, who approach everything with freshness, intensity and trust.

We are now raising *twenty-first-century children*, and are actually doing quite well – creating a kind of young person who is light years ahead of the young adults of thirty years ago. (Compare yourself at fifteen, say, with what fifteen-year-olds are like now!)

Raising kids is an ancient craft. To do it well you have to root out your hidden inner resources, as well as drawing on many outer supports. You adopt a kind of 'finding the way as you go' attitude – being willing to make mistakes and learn from them without hassling yourself unduly. That willingness to learn is probably what made you pick up this book.

You love your kids, you want to do your very best and you are willing to learn. You have all the ingredients to be a fine parent!

Two kinds of love

We love our kids. But love is more than just a warm feeling – it involves some skill. Family therapists recognize that parents need to have two core qualities. I call these *softlove* and *firmlove*. Both these kinds of love have to be activated in sufficient quantities in a parent's make-up, so that children receive the right ingredients to thrive. They are both available in *you*, but you may need some help to awaken them.

WHAT IS SOFTLOVE?

Softlove is the ability to be relaxed, warm and affectionate. It is the ability to stop your brain racing around, to trust your instincts and to fend off the many pressures put on you from outside so that you can *be there* for your child. When you can relax and be yourself, your lovingness will just naturally arise.

You don't have to force softlove, but you *do* have to give it space to grow. Not everyone was raised with softlove, and so sometimes we find it hard to activate. If you had rather distant or aloof parents, then you may feel tense or uneasy, rather than relaxed and loving, when you are around babies or toddlers. As men and women rediscover softlove, then many things will change for the better. Chapter 2 tells you how this is done.

WHAT IS FIRMLOVE?

Firmlove is the ability to be kind but firm with kids – to make clear rules and back them up, without getting angry, without being weak and giving in. It's the quality people speak of when they say, 'That person has backbone.'

Many people are confused about love because they think it is always warm and gooey. For instance, a father lends large amounts of money to his teenage daughter who 'forgets' to pay him back. This isn't love – it's just 'sogginess'. Firmlove means saying, 'Of course I love you. And you owe me £30. So no more loans till you pay me back!'

Firmlove is strength with a loving intention, as opposed to being cold and hard. Good parents are firm with little children often, because they love them. Often this relates to *safety* – 'I love you, and that's why I won't let you run off down the street.' Or *respect for others* – 'In this house people don't hit each other.'

Good parents are willing to be tough with their kids because they know this will help them to have a happier life.

FINDING THE BALANCE

No one gets it right every time. Giving softlove and firmlove to your kids is always a matter of finding your way, finding the balance as you go along. A parent who is kind and firm says things like – 'No, you are not going out in the rain and cold. How about looking for something interesting to do in the kitchen?' They are aware of their child's needs for activity – 'I understand you are bored – I'll help you find something to do.' But they are clear in their decision –'You have to stay indoors when it's wet.'

PROBLEMS ARE YOUR CUE TO ADJUST THE BALANCE

The so-called 'problems' that arise from time to time in every family are just your child's way of letting you know that the balance needs to change. For example, a little girl will get a tummyache because Mum and Dad have been too busy with the new baby. A boy will get into trouble at school to get more attention from his dad.

Sometimes you will have to develop new levels of either softlove or firmlove in yourself – more than you were ever given as a child – in order to help your child. That's why parenting is such a 'stretching' time – it takes you beyond all your previous limitations. This has to be a good thing, but you will need support and encouragement. The chapters coming up will give you lots of this, with many real-life examples to draw on for inspiration.

UNDERSTANDING YOUR LOVING STYLE

Lots of parents have asked for a simple way to measure how they are doing – and how they can improve. This simple questionnaire can help you to understand the two kinds of love, and to make your parenthood a more positive experience. Circle the number that best reflects your answer.

Softlove questions

1. I give my kids lots of hugs. I love to hold them and tell them how great they are.

   Not at all. 1 2 3 4 5 *Very much.*

2. I am a peaceful kind of person. I don't hurry. I can spend hours with my children just enjoying being together.

   Not at all. 1 2 3 4 5 *Very much.*

Now total the two scores above and enter your softlove total here.

SOFTLOVE TOTAL _______

Firmlove questions

1. I can be clear, strong and set rules, and get my children to follow them. The kids know when I mean business and nearly always obey.

   Not at all. 1 2 3 4 5 *Very much.*

2. I am calm and good humoured, so when I am being firm I don't often get really angry. I certainly never lash out at or hit my kids.

   Not at all. 1 2 3 4 5 *Very much.*

Now total the two scores above and enter your firmlove total here.

FIRMLOVE TOTAL _______

Now, enter your scores on the graph below.

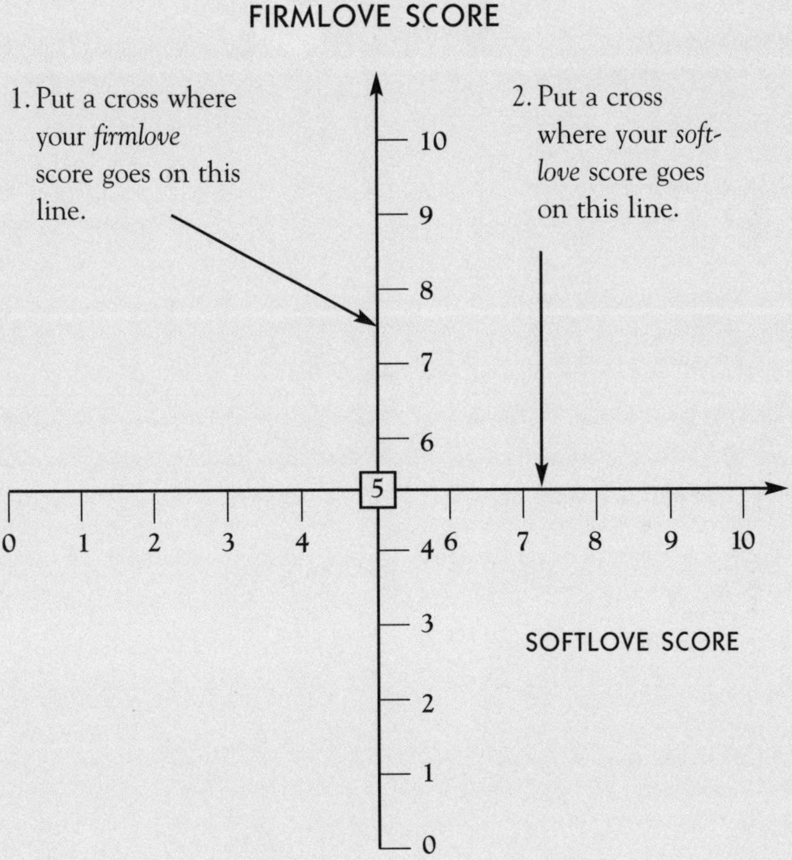

FIRMLOVE SCORE

1. Put a cross where your *firmlove* score goes on this line.

2. Put a cross where your *soft-love* score goes on this line.

10 9 8 7 6 5 4 3 2 1 0

0 1 2 3 4 5 6 7 8 9 10

SOFTLOVE SCORE

3. Draw lines across and down from your two scores and mark where they meet. This is your loving style result.

4. Look on the following page for an explanation of your result.

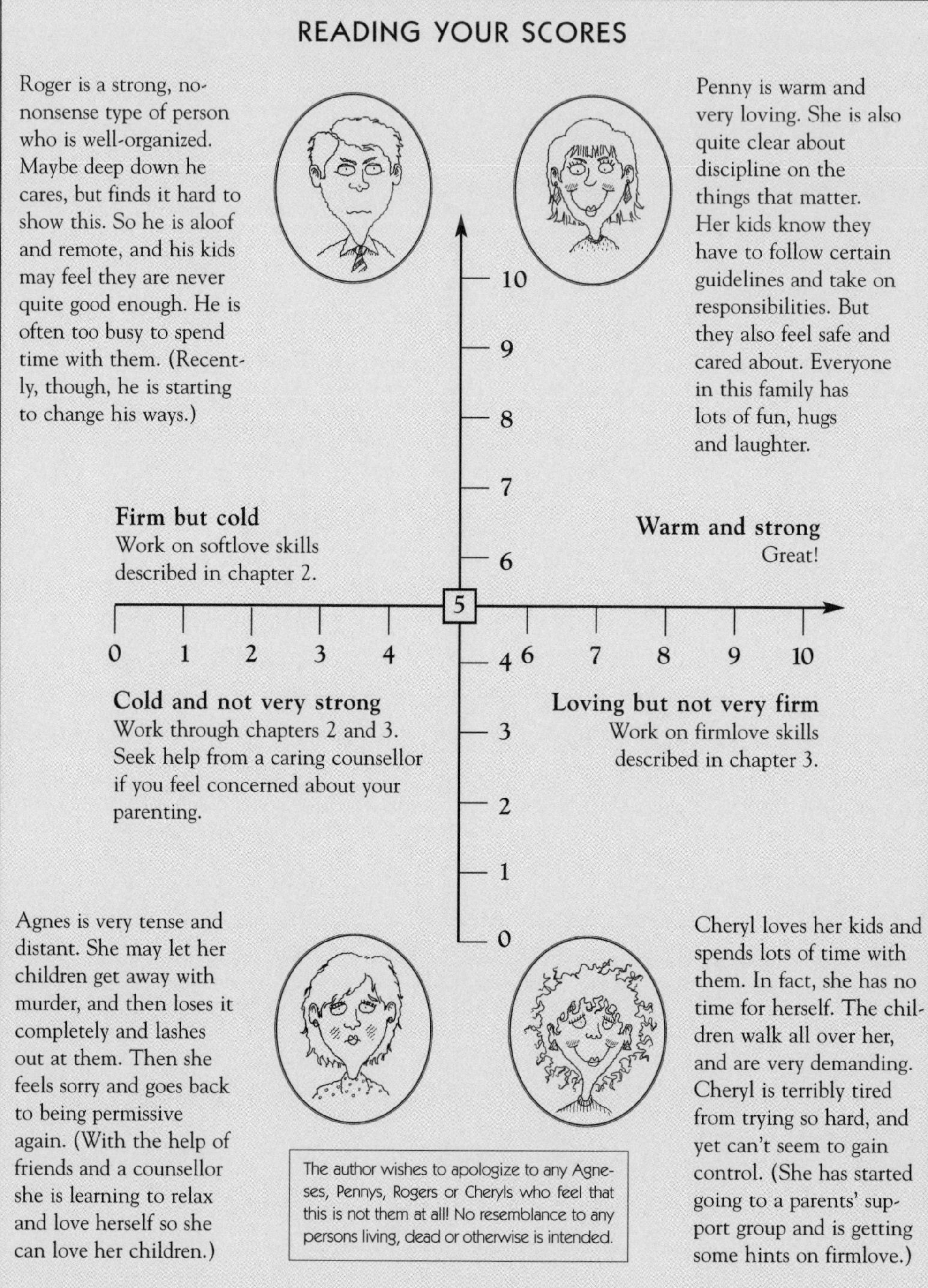
READING YOUR SCORES
Roger is a strong, no-nonsense type of person who is well-organized. Maybe deep down he cares, but finds it hard to show this. So he is aloof and remote, and his kids may feel they are never quite good enough. He is often too busy to spend time with them. (Recently, though, he is starting to change his ways.)
Penny is warm and very loving. She is also quite clear about discipline on the things that matter. Her kids know they have to follow certain guidelines and take on responsibilities. But they also feel safe and cared about. Everyone in this family has lots of fun, hugs and laughter.
10
9
8
7
Firm but cold
Work on softlove skills described in chapter 2.
Warm and strong
Great!
6
5
0
1
2
3
4
4
6
7
8
9
10
Cold and not very strong
Work through chapters 2 and 3. Seek help from a caring counsellor if you feel concerned about your parenting.
Loving but not very firm
Work on firmlove skills described in chapter 3.
3
2
1
0
Agnes is very tense and distant. She may let her children get away with murder, and then loses it completely and lashes out at them. Then she feels sorry and goes back to being permissive again. (With the help of friends and a counsellor she is learning to relax and love herself so she can love her children.)
Cheryl loves her kids and spends lots of time with them. In fact, she has no time for herself. The children walk all over her, and are very demanding. Cheryl is terribly tired from trying so hard, and yet can't seem to gain control. (She has started going to a parents' support group and is getting some hints on firmlove.)
The author wishes to apologize to any Agneses, Pennys, Rogers or Cheryls who feel that this is not them at all! No resemblance to any persons living, dead or otherwise is intended.

2

Softlove

Making contact with your child

All parents love their children.

The big question is: 'Will my love get through?'

It's dusk, and the bush around the lake is silent, apart from a distant lonely bird call. In a cottage by the water, a man and a woman are making love. They begin slowly, taking their time, enjoying the anticipation and the gradual falling away of tensions and cares. They are getting to know each other afresh, though they have been partners for many years now. After a time, the energy and passion begins to rise, her laughter mingles with his urgency, and soon they are both crying out in pleasure. Afterwards, there is a quiet resting and sleepy settling-together of warm bodies. Later, inside the woman's body, as they both sleep, a sperm finds its way to the waiting, moon-like ovum, and a child's life begins.

Loving the life inside you

How did you get to be a parent? You got pregnant – obviously!

Did you want to get pregnant? Who knows? Your body certainly wanted to. To your conscious mind, though, becoming pregnant can be a shock. Even the most highly planned pregnancy (not to mention the most totally 'accidental') brings this feeling. As you hold that little plastic test stick, you think 'Oh my!' The rollercoaster ride has begun!

Being pregnant confronts you with a choice. You can reach out with love to this new life inside you, or you can pull back in fear and caution. As your child grows inside you, is born and grows up, you will again and again have the choice to harden your heart and pull back, or to soften your heart and respond with the quality we call softlove.

Softlove – the capacity for tenderness, generosity and warmth – dwells inside every single person.

The softlove inside you may be strong like a fierce flame or it may stay like a tiny glowing spark, unnoticed, waiting to be kindled. Every new mother or father has this spark inside them. Researchers have found that when fathers are present at the birth, or get involved in the early care of babies, they become 'engrossed' in the child – deeply interested and deeply satisfied – wanting to spend more of their time around the baby, and wanting to become skilled in the baby's care. This is true whether or not the baby is their own biological child. The key is being there early.

A mother's body, if she is able to sleep alongside her baby from the very first, and especially if she is helped to breastfeed, releases powerful hormones called prolactins which actually make her want to mother. These hormones relax her and slow her down, giving her deep pleasure in being with her little ones. They prime her body for awareness and vigilance around babies. Whenever you feel clucky, drawn to anything small and furry, this is prolactin at work.

A note about breastfeeding. The evidence grows continually that breastfeeding provides nutrients and antibodies which make it far superior to artificial milk. Sometimes a mother has to bottle-feed through medical necessity, in which case it is important for her to bare her skin for the baby to feel while feeding. She should relax and make eye contact with her baby, and generally allow feed time to be a time of intimacy. We believe that breastfeeding is an art – mothers sometimes need understanding help to breastfeed successfully, and there are simple tips that can make all the difference. We recommend contacting the National Childbirth Trust or National Breastfeeding Alliance. They can provide wonderful individual help in most parts of Britain.

So the loving feelings are inbuilt and waiting to be awakened. Sometimes this happens easily and smoothly. Sometimes it needs help.

When you were a child, did you learn how to love?

If you didn't receive much love in your own childhood and babyhood, this can be one of the biggest barriers to letting your love flow – it may be that you didn't 'learn to love'. But it's never too late.

Our parents' generation cared about their children – but they didn't always show it, or say it very often. Many of today's parents were not raised with affection as babies and toddlers. In the 'icy 1950s', when medicine ruled birth and babyhood, it was considered 'spoiling' to be kind to a child. Parents were instructed to leave their babies to cry, or were afraid to feed them unless the clock said they could, or worried they would corrupt their children by cuddling them. Even today some authors and paediatricians advise letting babies cry out their distress alone in their room. What a disaster!

Jean Liedloff, in an article in *Mothering* magazine, concludes there are two basic feelings that all human beings need. These are to feel *welcome*, and to feel *worthy*. In the 1950s and 1960s, parents were often quite good at the mechanical side of parenting – feeding and clothing us and keeping us well. This was a pretty good start. But they often had trouble being warm or close, and in those days shame and blame were a big part of the discipline style. One could well grow up feeling unwelcome, and unworthy to boot!

One man explained to us that in his teens and twenties he felt a strong need to be around older, kinder people, just to bathe in the feeling of being welcomed in, given a smile, being asked about his day. Gradually, through doing this, he filled in the gaps in his feelings of welcome. After a time, he also knew that people liked his company, asked his opinion, told him their problems – and that made him feel worthy. In the end he became a psychologist!

An elderly friend told us that when she was a girl she used to feel very lonely and unloved. At midnight, when others were asleep, she would turn on the radio. The announcer on the late programme had a deep, friendly voice. She would stay awake to hear him wish everyone 'Goodnight and God bless.' Then she felt cared about and comforted, and slept soundly.

There were some plusses about childhood in 'the old days'. People tended to have lots of babies and lived close to their relatives, so older children, nieces, nephews, aunties and grandmas all helped with the babies. You got lots of practice at being a parent before you became one. (Today a quarter of new parents have never even *held* a baby until the day they first hold their own. No wonder they are terrified.)

To avoid parenthood becoming a big struggle you must get extra help for yourself – learning to receive love, so you can love your baby well. This begins very early. Research has found that the presence of a support person at the birth – someone who loves and cares about the mother – dramatically reduces the incidence of Caesareans, and of epidurals (and therefore forceps deliveries). Emotional care – in this case, of the mother – has real physical consequences.

Love is a real, tangible substance, and things go better when there is more love around. Once your baby is born, the best love people can give you is often practical: massage (for you), special meals, time and care, as well as help to protect your privacy. All of these kinds of loving can help to awaken your own loving capacities.

In short, if you had a secure and loving childhood, then things are likely to go well with your kids. But even if you didn't – and many of us didn't – then you can still turn things around for yourself and your children.

HEALING A MOTHER HELPS A SON

Esme, thirty-eight, had a difficult relationship with her teenage son. In fact, he was very depressed and possibly suicidal. We talked about how she and he got along. It was clear that almost every conversation they had involved her criticizing him. On the inside she cared, but on the outside she was cool and stiff, very unhappy in herself. As she felt safer with me, Esme confided that she rarely (if ever) hugged her son or touched him in an affectionate way. The very idea of touching him made her uncomfortable.

Emotional coolness on a mother's part is known to be a danger sign for suicide in teenage boys, especially if the father is also ineffectual or distant. So we made closeness our first goal. With encouragement, Esme began to reach out more. She practised casually putting a hand on her son's shoulder as she gave him his dinner, and giving him small compliments on his hair or clothes. After a week or two she moved up to giving him a brief hug when he left for school.

Esme found it hard to do these things, but she persisted. Then, one day in a self-development course she was attending, she was listening to someone in the group talking about their painful childhood. Suddenly she found she was shaking and shivering, and soon she was sobbing out loud. She was remembering being sexually assaulted by her father when she was about four. (Fortunately, her mother had left her father shortly after that.)

Esme had not so much forgotten these incidents, but had played down their importance to herself. Here was the reason why she found touch and affection difficult.

Through talking little by little in the group about her experiences, Esme learned to let others care for her, and she rapidly became a more outgoing person. All these qualities had been latent inside her, but were hidden by the fear of a little four-year-old girl whose trust had been betrayed. So helping her son turned into helping herself, too.

The power of touch

When you read the story of Esme and her son, did it surprise you that touch and affection could make the difference between a youngster wanting to live and wanting to die? Can touch really be that important?

On the surface, one wouldn't think that teenagers would be so concerned about their parents' affection. But a teenager was once a baby. And if they were not cuddled and stroked back then, it was a serious matter indeed.

Starved of affection, a little baby can literally die of loneliness. When a premature baby is stroked, growth hormones are produced. It's as if a baby decides life is worth living. When we receive loving touch our immune system fires up and resists infection much more readily. Haemoglobin (iron-carrying) levels in the blood increase dramatically.

Touch is an 'essential vitamin' for all mammals. When babies are born prematurely, they are often kept in incubators for many weeks. It has been recently discovered that if these babies are regularly stroked by their mother (or another loving person) reaching into the incubator and caressing their little bodies gently, they will gain weight 75 per cent faster than other babies who are not given this stroking. They are discharged weeks earlier, and save the hospital thousands of pounds.

FIND AS MANY WAYS TO TOUCH AS YOU CAN

There are many ways to show affection to small children – massage, stroking, patting, tickling, caressing, carrying, rocking, cuddling, brushing their hair, holding hands, giving rides, swinging, jiggling. Each conveys a different version of the same message – you are loved, you are welcome, you are worthy.

Sometimes older children go through a non-touch phase where they are establishing some independence. An experienced mother of teenagers told us that you still have to 'keep your arms open', because the time will come when they want to be hugged again.

Early problems and deprivations can often be healed later by gradually building up affection, as a child learns to trust. With sufficient time and care, fostered and adopted babies can overcome a difficult beginning. I have often seen and worked with adults who are healing babyhood neglect, and doing it successfully. But how much better to get it right the first time.

The power of praise

As kids get older, there are even more ways to make our love known to them. The most obvious way is with words. We shape their personality – by saying, 'You are beautiful, you are lots of fun, you are good to be around.' Kids become what we tell them they are.

Children need two kinds of telling. One kind is *unconditional* praise – this means that we let them know 'I love you because you are you.' They don't have to earn this love, and they can't ever lose it. Imagine how good this feels – to be unconditionally loved, just because you exist.

The second kind is *conditional* praise. This means that we tell them, 'I appreciate your actions.' For instance, we might say, 'I like the way you entertained your baby sister when the phone rang', or 'I really like your drawings', or 'You sing beautifully', and so on.

It's OK to tell kids what you don't like as well – as long as you don't call them names. 'You didn't pick up your clothes very well – I can still see eight T-shirts and 17 socks on the floor' is fine. 'You lazy little sod' is not so good.

Sometimes parents have to learn to *see* the positives before they can point them out. The power of our attention is a very powerful influence on our children. One of our teachers, Ken Mellor, puts it this way: 'What you focus on with kids is what you get.' Some families focus on illness, for example, and always have sick kids. Some focus on complaining (while trying to make everyone happy), and always have grumpy kids. If you look for negatives and always point these out (which some fathers are especially prone to doing), then the negatives will increase. If you let your children know that you notice when they act well, and comment on what they do that is great, then they will act great more of the time!

Quality of the week

Here is an exercise to try.

1. Choose the three qualities you most want your child to have (it could be anything – kindness to others, patience, gentleness, perseverance, cooperation, independence, creativity).
2. Take one of these qualities as your goal for this week.
3. Take note of every time they show this quality. Comment sometimes; other times just simply notice. Make no negative comments at all. By the end of the week, you can be sure this quality will be on the increase. Then move on to another. You can also let your child choose a quality, and notice it together through the week. Point out only when they *do* show the quality.

Time There is one essential ingredient for softlove, and that is being there; or, in other words, having time. However much you *tell* your children you love them, if you are not around enough, then your words will be a lie. With kids it's what you *do*, not what you say, that counts.

Lots of fathers today leave for work at 7.30 a.m. and return at 7.30 p.m. or later. These fathers are not likely to be successful as parents or, if they are, will only be so by making superhuman efforts on holidays and at the weekend. It isn't always their fault – the workplace is not yet a parent-friendly place. In the Stone Age, parents would often have to face a tiger or woolly mammoth to save their children. In the computer age, we might have to tell our boss to get stuffed! – equally dangerous.

It's not just dads – lots of mothers too are being conned by the comforting but largely false concept of 'quality time'. You can't have quality time with children 'to order', by schedule, on the dot. Relationships are a delicate business. If a woman has a husband who suddenly puts down the newspaper or turns off the TV at 10.30 at night, and gets all amorous after ignoring her all evening, she'll know the feeling that kids get when a parent lobs in for 'quality time'!

Certainly it's important to have special times. One easy and very powerful step to take is to sit down for a meal together each day, and switch off the TV or radio. It can be dinner, or even breakfast. Too few families eat together, yet it can be one perfect way to reconnect.

To a large degree, kids decide what they are worth based on what they are worth to you, and based on your enjoyment of their company. Imagine how good it feels to a baby or toddler to know that you value them more highly than almost anything else. As babies and toddlers, they *should* feel this way – not that they are 'the boss' but that their needs really count. This need reduces as they get older, but is still operating well into their teens.

Increasing your capacity for love

What is the quickest way to increase the love and positivity available in your family? You can start by learning a simple skill which all loving people have, often without knowing it. This is the knack of *living in 'present time'*.

Present time is where children live. To them, the future is impossibly far off. Kids live for today!

You were like this once. Can you remember when you were little, and a day seemed like a really long time? When six weeks off school at the start of the summer seemed like for ever?

An adult who can live in the now (at least some of the time) will be an instant hit with children. Old people sometimes have this ability because they've stopped rushing. Most parents (the people who most need to be) are hardly ever in present time. (As a young parent, I was a bad case of this. Whenever I was with my children, my mind would be somewhere else. My toddler son would give me a whack to bring me back to attention.)

Many people seem to have lost the knack of just being – especially if they live in cities, away from the rhythms of nature. Or, worse still, they think they are 'wasting time' or 'not achieving' if a day just drifts by. Yet, if you want to get through to your kids, whether to show them your love or to give them effective discipline, then you have to get yourself back into present time. Here is how to do just that.

GETTING YOUR BRAIN TO COME HOME

Most of the trouble we have in life comes from having a brain. Not just any brain, but a human brain – horribly prone to worries and abstractions which no dog, cat or budgie would ever waste a second on. (A mother once commented at one of my seminars, 'I worry if my children will ever get a job.' I asked how old her kids were and she said, 'Oh, I don't have kids yet!' She'd come along to my talk as a preparation for parenthood! Half of me thought, 'Great!', and half of me thought, 'This gal should be tenpin bowling!')

Our brain can make us miserable because it is always racing off out of control. So we miss out on what is happening right in front of us. There are three ways your brain 'races off'.

1. **Dragging around in the past.** Recalling the past can be very pleasant, but mostly people go into the past to rehash old regrets (what they missed out on), old guilts (what they shouldn't have done but did!) and old resentments (what others didn't do but should have).

   Going over the past, without changing any of it or having any new thoughts, is often a complete waste of time. Yet it probably occupies half of all human mental activity!

2. **Racing ahead to the future.** The future can also be a wonderful place to dream about, but most people just worry about what can go wrong. They use the future to practise 'worst-case scenarios' (a beautiful phrase!). Rent the video *Parenthood*, and watch for the baseball scene for a brilliant example of this.

The trouble with fearing the worst is that it either paralyses you, or else you react to things in an exaggerated way. You overlook the positive because it doesn't fit your plan of disaster. You miss the beauty of the roses because you are imagining yourself catching tetanus from the thorns.

3. **Wishing you were somewhere else** (or thinking you should be). Lots of people make themselves miserable by wishing they had made the other decision – taken that job, done that course, married the other guy or girl, lived in that other town, not had this baby. They are in one place, but hanker for another. Everyone does this at times, but sensible people use the energy to make changes, plan a holiday, or organize the future to more resemble the dreams they have. Others, though, just hanker. If only . . . aah, then I would be happy.

While we are busy racing off in our minds, we are making ourselves miserable, and we are missing out on our children.

Happiness, like a child, dwells in the present

In case you hadn't noticed by now, many of the best times in life just happen. Happiness often doesn't come according to plan. (Sometimes it does – the planned holiday or outing, a family occasion, a well-deserved trip to a restaurant or the movies.) But for every planned happiness there are ten accidental ones that will only happen if you allow them to – if you have enough time to appreciate them. Happiness is like a butterfly, waiting for you to stop still so it can land on your shoulder.

Magic moments

Life delivers us pearls of happiness when we least expect them. (Biscuit ads and new car commercials on TV try to capture these moments.)

You know the kind of thing – you're in a paddock or park with your children trying to fly a kite. It's cloudy. First of all the kite won't fly, then suddenly – it's up! The kids are running towards you with the kite behind. An eagle soars overhead. The sun is out suddenly and shining through their hair like golden haloes. Everything goes into slow motion, and are those violins you hear? Your partner smiles at you adoringly and you are suddenly and absolutely 'blissed out'. You wouldn't be anywhere else on earth!

Children store up these moments in their memory banks. At quiet times, or on long car trips, your kids will play 'Remember when . . . ?', recalling in detail the good times they had at that place and this. It builds their sense of belonging and their optimism for the future. Can you remember the really magical moments in your own childhood? I can remember a day at a football match with my dad, being kept warm inside his long overcoat. I can remember being held by my mother on the toilet when I was a toddler. She sat on the laundry basket opposite me, and I leaned on to her lap. Perhaps she was worried I would fall in. Whatever the reason, it felt nice. I remember making it last!

HAPPY ENDINGS – EVERY DAY!

One family we know has a five-year-old son and a two-year-old daughter. Each night, when they go to bed, these kids have a special ritual. Instead of reading a story, their mum or dad recounts the events of the day.

At the end of this story, they tell their child what was the very best part of the day for them. Then they ask their child, 'What was the best part of your day?' and listen carefully to what they have to say. Then they kiss goodnight.

It's a beautiful way to end the day, and a very powerful programming of energy towards the positive.

MADNESS RUNS IN FAMILIES

Family life these days often resembles organized madness. Parents rise before 6.00 a.m., gulp food, rush children to breakfast club, then to school, which takes them to after-school club. They pick them up after work, go home, cook tea, have 'quality time' (ho, ho!), do housework or office work brought home, and then collapse asleep after midnight.

Families today often own houses which require both adults working for thirty years to pay off. Some parents spend a quarter of their waking time sitting in a vehicle. Fathers work back at nights to pay private-school fees for children who hate school anyway, and have low self-esteem and drug problems because their fathers are never home. Marriages collapse from neglect and fatigue, but both partners blame 'communication problems'. Both partners get more quality communication with the tea lady! The British family seems to be dying of stress.

Being 'grounded' – a technique for calming down

Grounding is a powerful and simple way of getting your mind to settle down and be focused in the here and now. You can do grounding anywhere – driving a car, doing the dishes, walking down the corridor, making love. Here is how it is done.

Why not try this right now, as you read. Start by noticing your own body's 'inside sensations' – how your muscles feel, how your insides feel. Just notice these inner sensations, however slight. Focus on the inner sensations in your body, however vague they might be. Then start to notice what you are touching – your hands on this book (are your shoulders relaxed?), the chair pressing your back, the feel of your clothes on your skin. Just notice and intensify the sensations that are already there.

After a time, shift your focus to the outside. Look around you, smell and listen to what is around you. Become intensely aware of your surroundings. Literally 'come to your senses'.

You will notice the three distinct layers of experience: your *insides* (the sensations inside your body) – are you energetic, tired, relaxed, do you need to shift your position?; your *edges* – what you are touching, your hands on this book, the air on your face; and your *environment* – what is going on around you, what sounds, what colours, what action is around you?

As you notice these three zones of awareness without expecting or judging anything, you will become aware of several effects.

Your mind will slow down.

You will intensify the present moment – the beauty of it, the richness of it.

Your body signals come through more strongly, telling you there is something that needs to be done – stretch your legs, go for a pee, get something to eat! And so on.

At times, we are all troubled by an overactive mind. The best way to calm your mind is to give it something to attend to, something that is real and present. If you are driving a car, notice the feel of the steering wheel; if you are stacking the dishwasher, the feel of the dishes; if you are sitting with your child, the touch and temperature of their body against yours.

Unlike relaxation, grounding can be done anywhere in a matter of seconds. Using grounding takes practice and mindfulness, but it is as natural as breathing. Do it, and it will be totally reliable in improving your state of mind. Little children are usually already grounded. People who are very natural, rhythmic and down to earth are grounded and you can learn to be the same by just being around them. As you learn to be grounded more of the time, you will be less interested in being any other way. You will notice when you are getting too speedy or agitated, or depressed and stuck in your thoughts. You will be able to bring yourself smoothly back to the pleasures of the here and now.

Self time – what every parent needs

You can't give love if you don't have a clear sense of self. And a sense of self only comes when you give yourself space to be. Every day, you must keep some time just for yourself.

Some people get up early, or stay up late when everyone else has gone to bed, to get this time. Others make a deal with their partner to provide some self time for each other.

Self time is even more important than couple time, because you cannot connect with your partner until you have re-established a sense of self. Once you are happy in yourself, you will feel like being close to another person, but not usually until then.

Self time doesn't mean doing housework, though sometimes a big cleanup while the kids are minded can be very satisfying. It could mean time with friends. Watching TV doesn't do it well – you lose yourself rather than find yourself. Writing works very well – letters or a journal. Praying or meditation are good if you have a spiritual dimension in your life. Reading is pretty good. Lie in the bath with a glass of wine and a magazine! Head off to the bush, go into the garden, walk the dog. Everyone has their preferred way of having self time. The important thing is to do it and to schedule it regularly.

THE TREE OF (FAMILY) LIFE

You grow a family like you grow a tree. The roots are your own childhood and how you care for yourself. The trunk is your marriage or partnership, and your commitment to your kids. The branches are your actions based on choices you make every day. Your kids are the flowers and the fruit.

We live in as natural a way as possible, try to eat clean food, and work to make our world and neighbourhood better and safer places.

We dance around and play music and sing.

I protect my kids from exposure to dangerous people and violent or cheap media.

I hug my kids, and laugh and play with them often.

I work on my relationship and set aside time to get to know my partner. I do this for myself, for my partner and for my children.

We cultivate good friendships. Relationships with grandparents, neighbours, cousins and special friends provide a support network that I can confide in.

I am firm about my kids' behaviour, especially about respect for each other's rights and feelings.

I take steps to control how much my job intrudes on my family and my life.

I really like my children and enjoy spending time with them. They make me feel good (most of the time).

I'd rather be with my kids and be poor than have money but no time to spend with them.

I care for myself, and have time just to be me.

People were kind to me when I was young and I enjoy passing that on to the children of today.

OR I had a tough time as a kid, so I know it's important to 'water and feed the roots'. This will help me to do good things and to get good things and good care for myself.

Letting kids be kids

Once, long ago, I worked in a high school with drop-out children. One day during recess time, a group of my twelve-year-olds disappeared behind a huge stack of damaged furniture and I could hear giggles and shuffling sounds from deep in the heap. I suspected 'evil-doing' and crawled in to investigate. To my embarrassment, they were sharing their lunches and drinks in a kind of cubby house! They invited me to join them, but I just grinned and crawled ashamedly outside to the noisy world. I'd forgotten these were really just children, needing to play.

Perhaps the most serious and insidious harm that has been done to children in the last twenty years has been caused by the way we have taken away their childhood. There are several ways that this happens.

1. **A media bombardment** Horror, fear, grief and pain are compressed daily into our media news and our entertainment. TV has a little screen, so it has to have a big shock to hold our attention. The media blasts the same messages at toddlers as it does at sixty-year-olds. We heap our children with needless negativity which is not relevant to their lives and which they are in no way equipped to deal with.

2. **An overprogrammed life** Many families I know of spend evenings and weekends shuffling children to a range of sports, music, culture and supplementary learning venues. When all these 'extras' are combined with homework pressures, the average child has very little time just to be a child. We have the most overscheduled generation that ever existed. A solution to this might be a simple rule – one child, one activity.

3. **A competitive neurosis** Partly fuelling the second point is the feeling, easily caught by children, that life is a desperate race. So school takes on an anxious, performance-laden aura, even

from kindergarten. Instead of playing around, children join a competitive, organized, often expensive sport. Seven-year-olds are comparing their scores, worrying about their performances, praying they will make the team. This is madness.

4. **Overworked parents** Since we are so busy providing all these goodies, we have little time or energy to make contact. We become tense, snappy, and poor confidantes to our children. Feeling more guilty, we provide more possessions and experiences, and then have to work harder still to pay for them.

5. **An unsafe world** Whereas once children roamed the neighbourhoods and countryside of 1950s Britain, barely seen from breakfast till dinner, we now have to guard them carefully and protect them from traffic, strangers and crime.

We need a re-greening of childhood – a conservationist approach. We have to conserve the rare, natural and wild part of our children. This is an active process – cutting out and fencing off needless pressures and invasions. We have to 'de-pollute' our children's lives.

SOME POSSIBLE CLUES

- Have lots of time, space and materials for simple play. Plastic toys are cheap and clean, but mud and scrap paper, clay and water are the best toys. They give absolutely free rein to the child's own inclinations and imagination.

- Create healthy boredom – kids used to being entertained by computer screens, videos or schedules of 'educational' activity will take a little while to switch over to self-initiated play. You may have to resist 'I'm bored' for a time until they begin self-starting.

- Play is valuable in itself. Psychologists are discovering that this is the way children make sense of their world, act out concerns, overcome fears and learn to relate to others. Play is the source of all creativity and inventiveness. The great musicians, scientists, lovers, artists, and even managers, are the ones who have preserved the ability to play with their ideas and their work.

- You can play too – adults in crisis or transition often find healing in creativity, music, natural places, movement and the outdoors.

- Stop watching the evening news. Don't have a TV set running in the house – choose programmes and watch them, then turn the TV off. Give kids an hour a day and let them select what they will watch.

- Consider your whole lifestyle in this question. Do you really like where you live, how you live and the work that you do? Are there alternatives that would make your life more joyful, simpler, and yet still stimulating and rich? Perhaps we are living at a time when the whole world needs to 'wind down'. Children give you a good reason to do this.

Sometimes the arrival of babies in our lives kicks us into a frenzy of overactivity – renovating, working overtime to save for school fees, trying to provide what we think they need … when all the time what they really need is us!

My work with families in distress has given me an extra spur to not wasting my life with busyness – in one simple and trenchant way. Sometimes children die – and if we have missed out on the present while working for the future, then we will feel very bad indeed.

The best thing you can do for your children is enjoy them.

3

Firmlove

The secret of well-behaved children

It's a sign of the times that people are even using the word 'discipline' again. For those of us who came through the 1960s, this is an amazing turnaround. For about twenty years, the only place you heard of discipline was in ads for Madame Lash's House of Domination (whatever that was). But sure enough, as you leaf through family magazines and scan the bookshelves, discipline is back on the agenda. And not a moment too soon. When most modern house plans include a room called a parents' retreat, then it's clearly time to act. Let's reclaim the house!

Why discipline?

Uh-oh! You have just spotted them coming up the drive. Your best friend with her child – the toddler from hell. The kid who puts jam on your sofa, writes on the curtains and frightens pit bull terriers. Should you answer the door? Is there time to hide?

Discipline is a funny thing – you notice it most when it isn't there. Everyone knows someone with a completely out-of-control child and many of us have one of our own! Getting cooperation is a problem at times for almost every parent. Most British parents today are confused about discipline.

A small number of parents, on the other hand, seem to have it all sorted out. What is their secret? These parents call their toddler to 'come along now' and the toddler actually comes! You visit their house and your mouth hangs open. Their ten-year-old cooks tea for the family. Their teenagers phone to say they'll be home early. And these kids are not frightened mice – they're happy, optimistic and relaxed. How do these parents do it?

We all long to have well-disciplined kids for one simple reason – it makes life go more smoothly. Giving in to kids doesn't make life easier. Parents who are reluctant to set boundaries find that their kids just get worse. Without clear rules, you and your child may spend the whole day hassling and everyone feels bad at the end of it. Whereas if you have a discipline method that works quickly, problems are soon solved and you can get on with being happy.

There is more to it though. We don't discipline kids just for our own sakes – just to have 'law and order'. After all, if you want an orderly life, you don't have kids. The real purpose of discipline is to teach children to operate happily and easily in the world.

Without some parental firmness, children don't develop inner controls, and just keep on acting like two-year-olds, even when they are five, fifteen, twenty-five. Without inner discipline, a child's life is a mess. Parents who let children do as they like will severely disable them for living in the real world. These kids may end up unhappy, unemployed, unmarried, lonely, angry, and perhaps even in jail. A child who has been taught good self-discipline, on the other hand, learns how to negotiate the world and stay out of trouble, and so is really free.

Discipline is about getting along with yourself and with other people. After love, there is nothing more important you can give them than discipline. But not the kind of discipline that has often been implied by that word.

The approach to discipline we recommend is called *firmlove* – it is intervening out of love for the child. A parent using firmlove says, 'I love you, and that's why I will stop you behaving like this.' They combine love and firmness. They never hit, they never harm, they never blame. But they *are* firm.

'Stand and think' and 'dealing'

By now, you may be asking: 'What is this miraculous method of getting cooperation?' It's a good time to explain. Firmlove rests on two main techniques – the first is called '*stand and think*' and the second is called '*dealing*'. These methods are used from toddlerhood onwards, modified and developed as your child grows, and adaptable into adolescence and adulthood. In fact, the ability to 'stand and think' and 'deal' will become inner resources throughout your child's adult life, helping them to be mature, reflective and wise in all their dealings.

Let's find out how it's done.

LUCY MEETS HER MATCH

Twenty-month-old Lucy is playing with the power cords at the back of the stereo. She isn't doing this quietly or sneakily – she is in full view of her mother and father, who are deep in conversation. Her mother sees her and calls out, 'Lucy, hands off those power points. Come away and play with your toys.'

Lucy doesn't even budge. Her mother stands up and goes over to her – 'Lucy, hands off the power points, come over here.' Lucy looks up and gives the famous 'What are you going to do about it?' look. Her mother gives it one more try – 'Come away from the power points!' Lucy turns back to rewiring the stereo, muttering 'No, No, No!' under her breath.

Up until today, Lucy has never done anything this naughty. She has always been able to be diverted or negotiated away from trouble. Today, though, is her first real discipline experience. She is inviting her parents to struggle with her because this is what she needs.

It's time for action. Lucy's mother moves in briskly, grabs Lucy around the waist from behind with both hands, lifts her clear and takes her to the other side of the room where there is a free corner (every lounge should have a free corner). Lucy does not welcome this attention. She screams, yells, hits out and flails (which is why her Mum is holding her from behind!). Her mum continues to hold her firmly, safely, and tells her, 'When you are ready to calm down, you can come out.'

Lucy goes through many 'moves' that may be familiar to you – spitting, trying to bite, attempting to vomit her dinner up. Other children may hold their breath, call you names, and so on. Lucy has never been smacked and is not at all afraid. In fact, she is furious. How dare anyone interfere with her impulses! She looks to her father, who is standing back across the room. 'Daddy, helpa me!' Her father moves in and helps to hold her. He repeats what her mother has been telling her, in a calm, reassuring tone: 'You must stay away from power cords Lucy.' After what seems like ten minutes, but is actually about one minute, Lucy stops fighting and quietens down. Her mother has been saying to her softly the whole time, 'When you are ready to calm down, you can come out.' She now asks Lucy straight out, 'Now, are you going to stay away from the powerpoints?' 'Yeth!' she says.

Both parents stand back. 'Good girl,' they say, and watch to see what she will do. Lucy looks at the power points. She looks at her parents. She looks at her toys on the other side of the room. Then she heads over to the toys. And her mum and dad give a big sigh of relief and sit back down. In the weeks that follow, Lucy will try 'poking in the power cords' once more, and stop when spoken to.

She will be in and out of the 'thinking spot' many times before she is five years old – for all kinds of reasons. By the age of two-and-a-half she will usually go there when told to, and stand quietly and think over what she needs to learn. By five, she will have learned to think, to consider her actions, to account for the feelings of others, and still be a happy, spontaneous and easy-going child.

No hurt, no blame, no fear

For little Lucy, getting carried off to 'stand and think' was a surprise, but only her pride was dented – and only for a matter of minutes. With little children, we sometimes have to be physical, although always safe, and never scary. By carrying a screaming toddler away from a supermarket when they want to stay, restraining them from pouring soft drink into a sleeping dog's ears, breaking up a melee at the playgroup – we have to physically let them know 'that's not on!' With a toddler, we have to match words with actions. Move calmly without hurting (even when you are angry). In fact it's best to act early, long before you lose your cool. If you feel too stirred up, then forget the dealing, and just put them in their room till you cool down.

Soon you will be able simply to tell your child to go to a chosen spot in the room, to 'stand and think'. They will do so, knowing there is no option, but also knowing that it won't take long and isn't a big issue or a punishment – just the way forward through a problem. The emphasis is on the child finding a solution that is acceptable.

Beyond the old methods

There have been three main approaches to discipline over the past hundred years. Traditionally, people used hitting and hurting to frighten kids into behaving. Later, as hitting fell from favour, parents instead used blame and guilt to shame children into behaving. In recent times, people have used isolation methods such as 'time out'. As we know from sending adults to prison, isolating people often doesn't teach them much. So very little changes.

Firmlove goes beyond any of these, recognizing that discipline is about getting involved and teaching. Discipline is not about punishment. One of the great things about firmlove – using 'stand and think' and learning to 'deal' – is that you will never need to smack or hit your kids. Your children – and perhaps one day all children – can grow up without fearing their parents in any way. Can you imagine how good that would feel?

Firmlove means confronting children, certainly, and letting them handle some discomfort, but never inflicting pain. The aim of firmlove is simply to help children find better ways.

Let's look at another instance.

SEAN EATS HIS PEAS

Picture this. After four years of parenthood, Dave and his wife Louise decide it's high time they started to eat out again – with their little boy Sean in tow. They don't see why it shouldn't be possible to go to a nice place (one with tablecloths) and have a quiet meal, even with a child.

Plans are set in motion, and soon they are at the restaurant starting to eat their meal. But young Sean is not happy. Mum and Dad are looking at each other and not at him. He's bored. So he starts to flick his peas. His dad gives him a whispered caution – 'Stop flicking your peas!' But the way he says it sends another message – 'Please, not here, not in front of all these people.' Sean flicks another pea. His dad looks at his mum, who just looks right back. A lot is at stake.

Dave, the dad, gets determined. 'Eat normally, or you'll have to go and stand by the wall,' he says. Sean flicks another pea. Unbelievable! Boys always want their fathers to have backbone and to be true to their word. Dave is true to his – he marches with Sean (gently but firmly, as they say in the textbooks) past forty or so amazed diners, and leaves him in the corner of the restaurant. 'I'll come and talk to you when you look ready to sit and eat sensibly,' he says, and calmly walks back to his table.

Sean is a bit bluffed by all this. Soon his shoulders sag and he looks anxiously back across the room. Dave heads over and asks him, 'Are you ready to deal?' 'Yes.' 'What did you do wrong?' 'Flicked my peas.' 'What are you going to do now?' 'Eat normally.' 'OK. Well done.' And they walk back to the table.

A quiet kind of 'Yaay!' can be heard from tables all around the restaurant. Other parents, who paid babysitters £25 so that they could come out, can be seen taking notes on napkins – 'Are you ready to deal? What did you do? What should you have done?'

Had Sean been a child unused to 'stand and think' it might have been safer to take him out of the restaurant. He might have yelled and squirmed, and it would have been easier for his dad (and other diners) if he did this outside. If you do this with your child, don't leave him. Some firm talking, and the sudden change of environment, usually get Sean to realize that he will be better off settling down. Dave knows that this is a learning moment and that future restaurant meals depend on it.

IS IT NAUGHTINESS OR IS IT JUST ENERGY?

You only have to look at the human body to realize it is made for movement. In his beautiful book, *The Songlines*, Bruce Chatwin reports that Bushmen and women in the Kalahari carry their babies for 4000 kilometres on average before the little ones can walk by themselves.

Our bodies were designed to range over many kilometres each day. So adults or children will feel restless and bored just staying still. Worse still, playing a computer game or watching exciting TV will make kids feel quite twitchy – since these activities create adrenaline with nothing to expend it on. Kids *have* to get outside and get lots of whole-body exercise every day.

Occupational therapist Kerry Anne Brown believes that many later skills like reading, handwriting, posture, and coordination generally, depend on children running, climbing, bouncing, catching and expending huge amounts of energy in the early years of school. These early activities help organize the brain and build muscles to assist in the development of smaller movements like pen-holding later on. Even carrying little babies in slings and backpacks really helps – as do all those rough and tumble games that dads tend to play with little ones on the lounge floor.

A trampoline is a great investment, and any kind of climbing and swinging devices that are safe and well designed are worth their weight in gold.

Parks are also a big plus. Lobby your council to provide plenty of playgrounds in warm, sheltered spots, with shade from the sun and seats for adults. They should be near houses, not off in unsafe areas where young mums feel exposed. They should be well fenced, so you can read a magazine and not worry that your kids can wander off. Good clean toilet facilities would help.

When you are going up the wall, go to a park. I have spent many Saturdays on 'playground crawls' which, with occasional snacks and sandwiches, kept my kids totally satisfied on the cheap!

How to use the 'stand and think' and 'dealing' method

1. Preparation. Ask yourself, 'What's wrong here? What do I want them to do to fix it?' In other words, have a clear goal before you start.

2. Learning to stand and think is a skill in itself. With a young toddler, it is enough to take them to the spot you have decided on, and then stand back a little. Tell them, 'You have to stay there until you are ready to agree. You can come out when you've calmed down' or, if you are holding them, 'I'll let you go when you calm down.' At this age, as soon as they show signs of relenting, or mumble a few words of apology, let them out. Make it easy for them to get it right. For example, if they are throwing a toy at the wall and you want them to put it in the box, bring the box close.

3. As children get older (two or three plus), the conversation they have with you gets more important. Remember, they have to convince you that things are going to be different. They have to 'talk their way out' and convince you they can act differently. Another good name for this is 'dealing'. They are learning to 'deal'. Tell them their task – 'Stand there and think about what you did to get into this trouble. As soon as you've figured it out, I'll come and we'll talk about it.'

4. The dealing conversation. Ask them:
   a) 'What did you do?' Owning up to one's actions is important.
   b) 'What were you feeling or needing?'
   c) 'What should you have done to meet your needs?' Do they know a better way? Have you discussed this before? Perhaps you will need to teach them. For example, maybe they could join in a game others are playing, use a timer to share a toy fairly, put toys where a baby won't wreck them.
   d) 'What are you going to do in future?' Getting a commitment.
   e) 'Show me.' Go ahead and do it right now – get it right this time.

5. Aim for a happy ending. The beauty of 'dealing' properly like this is that the issue is resolved. You invest some time right now, and the problem need never recur (well, maybe once or twice). You'll know that this was successful because you end up feeling better, and your child feels better. Everyone is redeemed.

A whole new approach

This is a very different form of discipline from those that have been used in the past. When we look back to our childhoods, many of us associate discipline with feeling bad. The history of parenting since the Industrial Revolution has often been one of cruelty and distress for children. Many parents in the old days had little skill, and often simply repeated what was done to them (even though they had hated it at the time).

Once discipline is understood properly there is no need for hurt, shame or fear. The methods of firmlove are part of a breakthrough that is spreading all over the world. Good parents have intuitively found these approaches throughout history, but they have rarely been spelt out in a way that can be learned.

Firmlove methods are respectful of children, are non-violent, and yet clearly place parents in charge. We believe these methods can bring about a revolution in childrearing, making it easier and much more enjoyable to produce young adults who are strong, loving and safe.

The three tricks of getting cooperation

Many confrontations can be prevented. If you think ahead, you can often prevent situations from reaching confrontation level. To begin with you may need to use 'stand and think' at least a dozen times a day with little children. Soon, though, they learn to act on an early warning, or a count of '1, 2, 3'. A lot of the time, experienced parents find they can prevent problems by some forethought, and divert them when they do happen, so that confrontations are kept to a manageable minimum. This means that as children get to three or four, you can save your firmlove skills (and your energy) for the times once or twice a day when some important lesson needs to be addressed. Here are some ways to avoid problems – some of the time.

PREVENTION

A lot of kid trouble arises out of stress, fatigue and hunger.

Make sure you and your child have a good feed before going out, and stop for snacks regularly. Avoid really high-sugar or coloured foods, except as an occasional treat or after eating a meal. Most kids get zippy and harder to manage after a big sugar 'hit'.

Time your activities and leave out non-essentials, so that you are not pressured and having to race the clock. While raising toddlers, it's important to simplify your life. Little things suddenly take a lot longer to do, so do yourself a favour and allow for this.

Make your day ritualized and pleasantly rhythmic, so that kids get used to the routine. When getting ready for school or kindergarten, tell your kids to dress themselves first, before they eat breakfast. This avoids delays and hassles about dressing – hungry kids dress quickly without making a fuss. (To get them to eat a good breakfast is simple – just give them a light tea the night before. They will wake up ravenous!)

Make time at home happy. Have a fun time doing ordinary things – play boppy music while doing the housework. Slow down your expectations of perfection. Be a happy slob. You only have kids full-time for five years, and half-time for about ten years more. Why not enjoy it?

Sometimes little children who are restless just need more exercise – the modern world of small gardens, car seat belts, long drives and a dangerous environment are two-thirds of the problem. Sandpits, water play, room to run and climb make a huge difference. An exhausted child is a cooperative child.

DIVERSION

Often trouble can be avoided by finding a better way, striking a bargain, even bribery – 'I'll buy you some chips at the shop but you'll have to help me and get into your car seat.' A child fighting another over a toy can be offered a longer turn if they go second. Kids can learn to use a timer, to take turns, to play in such a way that both can participate. Sometimes boredom is the real problem, and you can increase the interest by adding a new element – and soon have them cooperating again.

A lot of 'naughtiness' is children just not knowing the right way to do things. Be prepared to teach rather than go on the attack when kids do something that isn't right.

For instance, picture a picnic table at the park. A couple of families are eating together. The eight-year-old boy grabs the last three pieces of chicken from the dish with both hands. Parent number one yells, 'Get out of there you guts!' and takes a swipe at him with a ladle. Good-humoured, but not likely to change his behaviour. Parent number two says, 'Hold on, you haven't checked if anyone else wants some. How about you take one piece and eat that. Then ask later if the rest is free.'

You teach your kids what good behaviour is. How else will they find out?

CONFRONTING

When you have tried all of the above and still your child is being difficult, then it may well mean that your child is asking for a confrontation. So why not give them one? Sometimes children set up conflicts from an inner need to experience safe, strong boundaries. At other times they just aren't able, without the help of our discipline, to handle a problem like sharing, waiting, not hitting, and so on. These are the times to use 'stand and think'. After all, a kid's life is pretty good, and it's not unfair if they have to cooperate sometimes whether they like it or not.

Whether the problem is sharing toys, being gentle, using words and not hitting, being patient, helping out, being obedient in an emergency, learning to join in a game, or whatever, 'stand and think' followed by 'dealing' helps them to stop their first impulse, think it through, and choose a course of action that is going to work. We are aiming not to 'shut down' their behaviour, but to make it more effective.

'So you wanted to join in the game the other kids were playing?' 'Yep.' 'So you threw stones at the other children?' 'Yep.' 'Did you notice that that didn't make them more friendly?' 'Hmm!'

From toddler to nice person in three short years

Raising little children is easier if you have a goal to aim for. You are working on producing, by age five or so, a civilized little boy or girl who can go to school, stay at a friend's place, mix well with other kids, and talk to adults in a comfortable way. They'll still have lots to learn, but will be well started.

In our illustration below, the Stone Age Toddler, accustomed to being the 'centre of the known universe', starts in the left-hand position. That's all right for a little baby, but not good as a life plan. The aim of the discipline game is to have children over at the right-hand

position by the age of five, ready to start school. Always remember that your child really wants to be kind, friendly and cooperative – but needs help to learn how. Expect lots of repetition, but also a sense of steady progress. And always have lots of fun and nice times in between the hassling.

All toddlers are difficult. You don't want to crush them just because they are showing strength. On the other hand, you don't want always to give in to them, because that teaches them that if they fuss and whine they will get their way. So it's a matter of being persistent and good-humoured.

Getting the firmlove attitude

The need for firmlove comes on in a big way when your child is around one-and-a-half to two years old. The arrival of 'naughtiness' can be disconcerting for the parent who just wants everything to be happy and gentle. Your baby shifts from an adorable if (demanding) little bundle to a mobile tank on legs.

It's a mental switch you just have to make. For parents of toddlers, firmlove involves realizing that, while you have just spent the last eighteen months trying to make your child happy, you suddenly have quite the opposite situation. You must now, if you are doing your job, make them quite unhappy – dozens of times a day at first, though hopefully only for a few minutes at a time.

> They will usually 'help' you with this by choosing to do something really 'unignorable' such as emptying the fridge or climbing into pot plants.

The attitude you need is tough on the outside, relaxed on the inside. Don't let them think they are cute when they are being defiant or mischievous. It'll take weeks to undo the damage. Drop your voice, look serious, but at the same time feel good that they are gaining lots of learning from having this discipline altercation.

> While softlove opens a child's heart, firmlove gives them more backbone so that they will be strong and clear in the world as they grow up.

What if I just give in for the sake of peace and quiet?

One day at the supermarket I decided that because my two-year-old daughter was fussing I would let her get off the trolley and walk around the aisles with me. This was a big mistake! She not only ran amok, she also expected the same thing for the next four shopping trips. Toddlers have memories like elephants!

Sometimes we want to take the easy way out. But this just teaches children to want more, and to whinge and whine harder. Think about it from the two-year-old's point of view. They have been, for the first year, the absolute centre of the universe. What they needed, they got. But now their wants have become more diverse and extreme. They don't just want to be fed, cuddled and changed. They want to dress the dog in your tights. They want to mix all the shampoo and conditioner into a slippery slide on the bathroom floor. They want to play in the traffic. You have to stop them, if only for their own good.

And it *is* for their own good. Because one of the most important lessons of life is being learned at this age – that, while you are loved and wanted, you are only one person among many and you have to get along with others too.

How soon does discipline begin?

Getting discipline to work smoothly is easy if you understand what to expect and what is going to work at different ages.

BABIES

Little Lukah doesn't need discipline. He is four months old. He is not yet able to crawl. He grins and plays with a rattle, and pulls things to himself. He also cries (many times a day) because he is a normal baby and that is how normal babies communicate their needs. His needs are simple – he cries when he is hungry, he cries when he is lonely, he cries when he is wet, he cries if his tummy hurts, and he cries when he is

HAVING LIKEABLE KIDS, ONE GOAL AT A TIME

Jodie, a participant in one of our courses, was very frank. 'I don't like children,' she said. 'I've got three, and what I've found is that I just don't like kids after all!' This is a problem, because if Jodie doesn't like her own children, how will anyone else like them? It's her job to turn them into kids that are likable.

To help her, we get more specific. What changes will each child need to make so that Jodie can like them? We make a list.

1. Her two-year-old will stop hitting and biting.
2. Her four-year-old will stop whingeing and complaining.
3. Her five-year-old will learn to carry out instructions the first time he is asked.

Softlove comes before firmlove, and we realize that Jodie is quite exhausted and will need time out for herself one day a week, as well as extra help from her husband. They resolve to give each other more care and attention, and practise firmlove skills together so they can back each other up. He will reduce his working hours from fifty hours a week to forty-five, so as to do this. Having well-behaved kids will make him happier to spend more time at home.

When we see Jodie six months later, she is looking much more relaxed and peaceful. Her life is still hard work, but she is being gentler on herself, and feeling much more successful with the kids.

bored. That adds up to a lot of crying, but if his mum and dad are on the ball they soon know what is probably needed and are in there at the first whimper to fix him up.

Lukah's dad explains that he was a very high-need baby: 'The big problem was getting him back to sleep – I had to put him on my shoulder and go for a walk around the neighbourhood. Once, at about 4 a.m. the police pulled me up because I looked like a burglar with a swag bag.'

Babies can be hard work, but they are not being naughty – they are just trying to let you know their needs. They don't need discipline, just lots of understanding. And what parents need is sleep.

TODDLERS

Babies' abilities quickly grow until soon they are crawling and then walking about, grabbing and pulling, chomping and poking everything in sight. The whole bottom half of your house is their domain. They are also discovering the use of words to make things happen – 'Bottle!' 'Gimme teddy!' 'Hugga me!'.

With their new skills and mobility, your child is starting to do things and want things which you can't possibly allow. So 'misbehaviour' emerges for the first time. A little baby doesn't deliberately misbehave – but a toddler is a different matter. Your toddler will walk over to the forbidden place or thing, and flash you a grin that says, 'Whatya gonna do about it?' You say, 'No,' and they smile, 'Oh yeah? Stop me.'

Toddlers choose exactly what will 'get your goat', because deep down they are wanting to be stopped. This is an unconscious message saying, 'I need some limits, Mum and Dad. Please stop me going berserk.' (Teenagers too send this message, and we'll talk about them in a little while.)

It isn't all pure rebellion (though some of it is). Sometimes a toddler will just find it too hard to handle the demands of day-to-day life. Sometimes they will just be tired or hungry, and best put down for a sleep or given a snack – their mood will soon improve. Perhaps they will not want to be strapped into their car seat to go to the shops when something good is going on in the yard. Or they will want to crawl across the dinner table to sample what's on their big brother's plate.

A kind parent uses all kinds of tricks to cajole a kiddy along, and a lot of the time this is just what is needed. For instance, one mother saved me a lot of trouble by explaining that if you give your toddler something delicious but time-consuming to eat when you go into the supermarket, they will sit happily in the trolley for twenty minutes. All the same, there will still be times when a child just has to be confronted and do what they are told, because 'I say so'. This age is definitely the firmlove fiesta.

PRESCHOOLERS AND OLDER CHILDREN

As children get beyond the toddler stage, you'll need to use 'stand and think' far less often (thank goodness). Children will 'deal' with you straight away most of the time. Listen to their side of the story – what they were feeling or needing – as it might well be valid. If they can make a good case, then obviously you don't make them do things just because you want to be 'the winner'. They will learn that it's OK to have feelings or needs, but that sometimes they can't get what they want or maybe they can if they go about it in a more acceptable way. Always find out from them what they were feeling (the feelings that led to them playing up), and use firmlove in a kind way so that they know you really want to help, not just persecute them.

TEENAGERS

Despite what people think, adolescents are generally beautiful, cooperative, interesting people. But they are still needing lots of involvement, and this includes some confrontations from time to time. It isn't right to use physical force with teenagers in any way, unless things are severe and you have professional help. So 'stand and think' becomes 'sit and talk'. For example . . .

What time did you come in last night?

Uh, about one?

That's what I noticed. When did you agree you would be in by?

I said twelve, but it was hard to get a lift. The others wanted to stay.

So you couldn't get a lift and that made you late?

Yeah. Can I watch TV now?

Not so fast. How come you made a promise to me that you couldn't keep?

Well, I can't make the others bring me home!

Did you know that could happen when you made the promise?

Uhh, well, I didn't know.

So you made a deal you couldn't really keep.

Uhh, well, I guess so.

So how can we fix that in future? You do want to go out in future?

Huh! Yes I do!

. . . and so on.

In the brain of a teenager around thirteen years of age, everything is suddenly rewired. Puberty is setting in, and it makes them like a newborn baby. They can become forgetful, disorganized and slightly 'out of their tree'. On the plus side, the changes combine to make them very 'soft'. Thirteen-year-olds can be trusting and affectionate – so it can be a chance to get close to them and rebond. Especially if you were hassled and busy when they were babies, this can be a time to build greater closeness.

Enjoy this time, because the 'dopey thirteens' soon give way to the 'cyclone season' of the fourteens. Fourteen-year-olds can be like emotional two-year-olds – testing limits, wanting to struggle with you and needing you to struggle back. The last thing you should do is ignore them. They are wanting independence but needing to learn to be responsible and careful – a peak time for parenting input.

So for fourteen-year-olds firmlove comes into play once again, only this time about different issues – what time to be home at night, picking up your clothes, cooking meals for the family and keeping promises and agreements. The methods of firmlove you use with teenagers are different from the ones you used with toddlers, but the principle is the same. 'I will be firm with you, so you will learn to be a responsible person and know how to handle the real world' is what you are thinking. 'No dishes, no dinner!' is what you are saying.

Teenagers are a big topic, which we can only touch on in this book. It is clear, though, that by getting softlove and firmlove working well with little children and school-age children, you will have a good foundation for handling adolescence when it comes along.

Questions parents often ask about 'stand and think' and 'dealing'

Q. ***What about a child who has not been disciplined much before, and is very naughty? I've tried lots of things and nothing works.***

A. If you are introducing 'stand and think' to a child who is very disobedient, then wait till you are ready. Make sure it is a good day when you have someone there to help you and are clear in your mind what you want to achieve.

When and if a problem arises, give the child the chance to fix it. If they don't do that, explain that this will be a new way of dealing with problems. Walk them to the spot you have chosen and say something like, 'You [threw the cake, hit your sister] and you have to stand here and think about it – why you did it, why it's a problem and how you can fix it.' If they try to move away, then hold them firmly, but safely without hurting.

Expect some dramatics. It's a bit of a shock to a child used to running amok. So decide to 'stay with it' even through their loudness and struggling.

Always be firm without hurting. Say to them, 'I will let you go when you stand still', then do it immediately they comply.

Keep it simple and make it winnable. The first time, be happy with a small improvement – a quick 'Sorry' or a token effort is enough the first time.

They will calm down.

They will cooperate.

They will be praised for the new behaviour.

And you will have a little lie down afterwards if you need it!

Next time, it will be a lot easier.

Q. Should I hold them in the thinking spot if they won't stay there?

A. If they are little (one-and-a-half to two-and-a-half) allow them to sit or lie down – as long as they stay put. Stay close by and catch them and put them back if they try to 'escape'. You will probably only need to do this once or twice. When they are ready to talk, ask them to stand up and turn around to talk to you. An older child should stand quietly facing the wall, not propped up against it. Physically this keeps the child's attention on the one thing they should be thinking about. They literally aren't squirming around the problem, but are 'standing up' to the task you have given them. Explain that only when he or she does this will you be willing to talk to them.

Q. How old should a child be when you use this method?

A. For you to be using this method, a child needs to have a certain amount of understanding and language. If they can say 'Sorry', 'Not hit' or 'Hands off video' then they've got the message. Tell them they can come out now and get on with doing something pleasant. You can cuddle and calm them afterwards, but don't make a big fuss. The aim is to let it go and get on with life. Until a child has these talking skills, you have to use more baby methods, like diversion!

Q. Why stand up, and why use a corner?

A. This is for simple reasons. It cuts out other distractions and helps the child to focus their attention. It is boring to face the wall, and your legs get tired in a minute or so just standing still. It isn't meant to be either painful or embarrassing. The aim is to get the child motivated to solve the problem and get out of there. Tell them, 'You don't have to feel bad, you're there to think about what you should have done. As soon as you have figured it out, we'll talk and you can come out.'

Away from home, or once your child is really used to standing still when told to, you don't need a wall or corner. You can simply say, 'Stand there and think', in any location.

Q. My child says he's sorry, and then does it all over again.

A. The older they get, the more they try you out – it's the sign of a smart kid. Expect the following confidence tricks:

- I can't stand and think – I have to go to the toilet.
- You don't understand me.
- You don't love me.
- I can't remember.

This child is *not* sorry.

This child is ready to deal.

Don't be fooled. They have to convince you (before you let them out) that they really are feeling sorry, and really are going to change. Through watching their body language, and through being alert during the dealing conversation, you will soon know if they are genuine.

Q. Can schools use this method?

A. Yes, but only with some important modifications. 'Stand and think' would be humiliating in front of peers other than brothers and sisters in a family setting. Many primary schools we have consulted with now use a 'thinking place' which is a chair, mat, stool or beanbag. The thinking place isn't especially conspicuous, and shouldn't have a humiliating name like 'naughty chair'. The thinking place is used in the same way – to remove a child from the action, give them time and motivation to think, and keep them close by where you can see from their body language if they are ready to 'deal'.

And always a teacher or principal should deal with them soon. It isn't a sentence they are serving. Kids who play up do need your attention, so give it to them, through dealing with what happened. Remember also to give them attention when they are doing the right thing.

Often in school, a round-table discussion with affected children can be held on a mat or at a table. Problem-solving skills are as important as the three Rs.

What about the old ways of discipline?

There has been a gradual evolution of discipline techniques in the last fifty years.

HITTING AND HURTING

This was the old way. It made children frightened, it eroded any loving relationship, and it taught children that it's OK to hit if you are bigger. Children who were hit became fearful or broken-spirited, or they got angrier and struck back. Sometimes when these children grew up, their own children, wives and others copped the anger that had been stored in their bodies. Violent methods are harmful and have no benefit. In some countries, they are against the law.

SHAMING AND BLAMING

When parents rightly began to reject hitting and smacking in the 1950s, they sometimes had no other tools to put in their place, and few skills in communication. So they often used shame, fear, blame – calling their children no good, and a million other names. The result was a damaged self, a wounding of the spirit. Shaming and blaming were often a failure as discipline too, because children became what they were called – lazy, stupid, selfish, fat, whatever. Kids who were shamed went one of two ways – either depressed and guilty, or rebellious and angry.

REWARDS AND CONSEQUENCES

A good example of these are star charts, where a child gets stars for good behaviour, usually building up to some reward at the end of the week or when they have enough stars. Star charts can work well because they help parents focus on the positive, and they help the child have smaller goals to aim for. With some children this can make a lot of difference.

Pocket money in a small quantity, some jobs which you just 'have to' do as your part in the family, and extra pay for doing extra jobs, is a mix of rewards which many families have found works well because it resembles the real world.

Similarly, 'natural consequences' work by letting the child have the problem they create – changing the sheets if they wet the bed, getting into trouble if they are late for school, and so on. As children get older, they are more and more able to learn from the results of their actions and it is important that parents allow this to happen. Natural consequences aren't enough on their own – for example, the consequence of running on the road would not be a good idea.

TIME OUT

Time out has become a popular recommendation of parenting experts. It means sending your child to their room, usually for about five minutes, to cool off. It has literally saved a lot of children's lives, because it gives parents time to cool off too. So it is a coping strategy, and useful to almost everyone at times. I use it myself with a toddler when I am hot and bothered and just want some peace for a few minutes. But in itself time out is not a discipline method because it doesn't involve teaching or thinking about change.

Here are some examples of what parents tell us about time out: 'It doesn't work because my child has fun in their room, they have so many toys!' or 'He smashes the room up, breaks things, and sometimes gets out of the window' or 'It works well for me – mainly as a chance to cool off. But it doesn't always change the behaviour. She often just does it all again ten minutes later.'

The key differences between 'time out' and 'stand and think' are:

1. 'Stand and think' is quicker. When the child is in the corner in the same room with you, you are able to see straight away when they have finished thinking about their behaviour. It encourages rapid resolution.
2. There are no distractions with 'stand and think'. The child stays put until they do the thinking they need to do. It keeps the problem with the child.
3. 'Stand and think' isn't a punishment. It's a thinking and teaching time. It doesn't create resentment. The child can end the process by cooperating at any time, and so is usually out within a minute or two.
4. 'Dealing' creates closeness, not distance. Naughty kids don't need isolation – they usually need more intense contact. The dealing conversation shows that you care, and you want to help them solve their problems.

We recommend that you only use time out if you feel you are in danger of hitting your child, or otherwise really need a break. In fact, you can use it preventively by saying, 'I want us both to cool down now. Please go to your room and play quietly.' You may wish to have a 'dealing' conversation afterwards, so that you know something has been changed.

Helping older children with moral decisions

Some childhood dilemmas aren't so much discipline questions as values questions. You want your child to decide for themselves what is the right thing to do. You can't make kids take on your values. But you can help them figure out all the angles about their behaviour. In the long run, this means they will do the right thing when you are not around, because they believe it is the right thing.

Sara, aged nine, was asked by a friend to go to her sleepover. She happily agreed. Her friend, a shy girl, was really pleased that Sara had accepted – there were only three girls attending.

Then, out of the blue, Sara was invited to a church camping weekend by another friend – but it clashed with the date of the sleepover. Sara really wanted to go on the camp, but it meant breaking her acceptance of the sleepover. Her parents didn't force her to keep the agreement – that would have just led to sulking. But they discussed the two parts of the problem with her:

1. Respecting her friend's feelings.
2. Keeping an agreement.

These were important principles. Sara's parents gently pointed out that 'something better has come up' is no excuse for disappointing someone who is counting on you. They also said it was Sara's decision, and they wouldn't hassle her once she had decided. Sara reluctantly declined the camping trip, and had fun at the sleepover. Her parents felt really proud of her for showing so much character.

Children and teenagers won't always make the decision you are hoping for. But making mistakes is part of the lesson. Also, it's just remotely possible that you might be wrong and that they might be right – a sobering thought!

Should I smack? – an important decision every parent has to make

It's getting dark, and the road is heavy with traffic going home for the night. People hurry along the footpath and a light rain has begun to fall. A little child's yelling catches my attention – a young mother is talking at a public phone outside a shop, at the same time trying to keep her toddler in check. He wants to run and play at the kerb, where rainwater is gurgling and splashing. But the cars and trucks are dangerously close by. You can feel her frustration – she is alternately raging angrily with whoever is on the phone, then shouting at her youngster that she will 'teach him to behave'. He whinges and struggles to pull free. Then it's all too much. She drops the phone, grabs the neck of his tiny jacket, and gives him a backhanded blow across the face that makes his head spin.

ATTITUDES HAVE CHANGED

It used to be an everyday event, forty or fifty years ago, to see children being beaten by adults. People did it in public, and nobody much batted an eyelid. Attitudes to hitting children have changed, just as they have changed to men hitting women. Today, a bruised child is a police matter. Eighty per cent of parents say they still smack their children occasionally, but most would prefer not to.

There are still many people, though, who advocate a smack as a way to get quick results. Perhaps it's time for us to make a personal choice about what happens to our kids – especially now that better forms of discipline are available to us. We believe that if parents knew of a better form of discipline, they would never smack again.

Are beating and smacking the same? Isn't smacking just a little bit of needed discipline? Often when I give a talk about discipline, someone will come up to me and say, 'I got plenty of hidings when I was a kid, and they never hurt me!' My guess – based partly on the very passion with which these people speak – is that it did hurt them, and it still is hurting. Pretending it didn't hurt is the child's first defence against humiliation. And the anger they hold inside comes out later in many different ways.

It's time we were more honest about this whole issue. From a child's viewpoint, smacking is scary and humiliating. From a parent's point of view, it is risky. Risky because there isn't any clear-cut point where a smack becomes a hit, and a hit becomes an angry venting of parental frustration. How do we know how much is enough? Can we honestly say when we are hitting for the child's 'benefit', and when it's just to make us feel better? Or to get revenge? Can we honestly say it's just the child we're angry with, and not a lot of things rolled into one?

The bottom line(!) is that smacking really doesn't work, except in the very short term. It eats away at love and trust – so children get crankier still. I have seen lots of children – who defiantly say, 'It didn't hurt! I don't care!' – learn to become immune to it. The parents who lay into their children in the street or supermarket are clearly losing control of their children, not gaining it.

WHY DO PARENTS SMACK THEIR KIDS?

The fact of it is, if we're honest, we hit children because of our own needs. We are scared of losing control over them. Or, often with young children, our nurturing energy just runs out. We feel exhausted, sleep-deprived, we never have a moment to ourselves. The slap is just our inner self striking back, saying 'I've got needs too.' It can be a self-protection instinct – they've just jabbed you in the eye as you put them in their car seat, or banged you with a spoon as you straighten their bib.

At this age, children can't always understand or notice our feelings or our words to them. Yet we feel a strong urge to make an impact, to have an effect on their behaviour. So smacking or hitting them to 'get their attention' is a natural urge. We need to resist this urge, and can do so if we improve our skills in connecting with children and making them take notice.

Some smacking advocates are compassionate and concerned people. They often argue that, if not controlled early by a light tap, children will become even naughtier, until their parent loses all patience and gives them a real hiding. Their theory is that little hits prevent big ones. However, our experience is that parents who give little hidings also give big ones – the little hidings soon don't work. Kids get resentful, they hit their own brothers and sisters, or hit you back. It's important to draw the line, and the realistic place to draw it is back at square one. If we decide *never* to hit our children – as I and many people I know have done – then we are committed to finding better ways.

DISCIPLINE WITHOUT SMACKING

We do have to discipline children. And words alone are not enough with very little ones. It's certainly necessary sometimes to hold and restrain little children to help them to calm down and behave. This can be done quite safely. 'Stand and think' has been adopted successfully by thousands of parents. It's a matter of training your child as they grow up. And there will still be 'impossible' times in the rain in the street, where it's just a matter of 'pick up and carry'. You have to keep your sense of humour. It's lucky toddlers are small – it makes them portable.

By the time adolescence comes along, there should never be any need for fear or intimidation. If kids run away from home, or are violently defiant, this almost always means that communication has broken down years back, and parents have been relying on aggression rather than a mixture of love and assertiveness.

Many people block out the memory of the pain they felt as children – and so go on inflicting this pain on their kids. As a counsellor, I know what pain is involved. I have heard too many people talk – with tears in their eyes – about the humiliation and fear they felt when a parent went out of control. My patients show me the broken blood vessels in their legs from being 'smacked' as children. Hairdressers tell me many of their clients have nicks and bare spots and scars under their hairline from blows on the head when they were little. The scars are even bigger on the inside – if a child cannot feel safe and secure with its own parents, how can it feel safe in the world?

There's another reason to stop hitting children. Evidence is mounting that children who feel safe with their parents will tell their parents if something is wrong – for instance, if they have been sexually assaulted. When parents routinely use fear and shame as discipline tools, then children will feel unsafe to tell, in case they get the blame. Kids who are never frightened or harmed by their parents will always see their parents primarily as protectors. They will feel safer to say, 'No – I'll tell!' to somebody else, and avoid abuse in the first place.

MAKING THE DECISION

We think that it is time for us as parents to abandon hitting as a way of controlling children.

The first step is simple. You make a personal commitment never to hit a child again. The automatic effect is that you become committed to finding non-violent discipline methods that work. Such methods exist, and are able to be mastered.

While raising our first child, we found ourselves giving little smacks for certain behaviour – things like touching the heater. Being a strong-willed child, our son was not impressed by this and made a habit of repeating the behaviour. We found that we were miserable about making him cry, and we weren't teaching him much either. So we began to search for alternatives. We discovered that some parents *never* smacked their children, and that in fact there were whole countries where it was illegal to smack a child. We also learned the firm and clear forms of discipline taught in this book, and used by thousands of parents around the world, and began putting them into practice at our place. We are eternally grateful to have found a better way.

We are all yearning for a peaceful world – where conflicts can be negotiated non-violently. We need to start at the beginning. If we can't manage it at home, we will never manage it in the Middle East.

If you find yourself in agreement, you can make this commitment too. Your child will come to know that their mother or father will never, ever, physically harm them. That they are safe in their own home. What a beautiful way to be.

OUR HOME IS A NO SMACKING ZONE

Conclusion By using firmlove methods, you can win both ways. You can give up on smacking and blaming, which no one really enjoys. And yet you can have a household where the adults are in charge, and the kids do what they are told when necessary. Your kids will still be normal – two-year-olds will still be hard work, and fourteen-year-olds will still be cyclonic. But by knowing how to respond you can address these stages confidently and clearly, and then get on with the enjoyable and pleasant parts of family life.

Remember – always and only do what works best for you. 'Stand and think' and 'dealing' are just two more possible strings to your bow. As this letter from a family indicates, they can make a lot of difference:

Dear Steve and Shaaron,
We attended your seminar in October, and thoroughly enjoyed the session. I still keep in touch with another lady I met there.
Your seminar came at an appropriate time because we didn't want to beat our son Carey, but didn't know what to do. Now Carey (twenty-eight months) stands himself in 'the corner' and says 'I'm thinking about it' and the tears in our eyes are from joy – he's so cute!
Marion and David

4

Who will raise your children?

Taking care with childcare

It's 9.30 in the morning when the phone rings. On the line is a young professional woman whom I know only slightly. She is in tears. She has just left her four-month-old baby boy at a child-care centre for the first time, and is now sitting at her desk on her first day back at work.

The baby was distressed to be left, she was anguished to leave him. She can't concentrate on her work – all she can think of is her baby, who has scarcely been away from her in his whole short life. What should she do?

Doing what your heart says

Many people would say to the young mother returning to work, 'What's the problem? The child will soon settle down.' After all, this can happen with a five-year-old, too, on their first day at school, and they are usually soon over it and settling in happily. Shouldn't she just put it out of her mind and concentrate on her job and her workmates?

As we talk it over, it emerges that it isn't just a problem of a tearful parting. This young woman has a deep ambivalence about returning to work.

We discuss the pressures on her, trying to separate what are her own feelings and what are the wishes of others around her. Many of her friends have their babies cared for in creches and are working. Her husband wants her to go back to work – the money will be welcome. Her employer wants her back at work – she has only been away five months in total.

But as she talks it's clear that she is not happy. What she wants is to be with her child. Gradually, she begins to settle on what she will do. She decides to meet with her boss and explain that she has changed her plans, to apologize for this, and thank him for being understanding. After negotiation with her boss, she in fact takes a whole further year off, and then returns only part-time. She's lucky – to be a skilled person, and to have a partner whose income can support the family – so that she can choose to do this. She is enormously relieved to be following her own heart, and not the 'shoulds' put on to her by society and those around her.

Childcare – a new invention

From time immemorial, most children have been raised close to home by a combination of their parents and close relatives, in a village or neighbourhood setting. So the work (and the pleasure) of raising children was shared amongst those who loved them. Throughout the non-industrial world, even today, children and adults spend their days together. You will see mothers at work with babies in slings, and little children accompanying men to work in the fields. It is only in the Western world that we shut our children (and our old people) away from the mainstream of life.

One hundred years ago most men worked with their wives and families close by – the vast majority of British men worked within walking distance of home. Then, with industrialization men began to travel to distant work leaving women and children, often isolated and lonely, at home. In the 1960s women decided they wanted to work too, and joined men in a flight from the home.

Reduced wages, single parenthood and unemployment have meant that many women *have* to work, as well as raise a family. To deal with this, there has been a rapid upsurge in childcare provisions of various kinds. Today, we talk of the childcare 'industry' and finding suitable childcare is a subject close to the heart of almost every parent.

So today's parents have an option that in the past was only available to the extremely wealthy. We can pay professionals to mind our children all day. If you can overcome the problems of waiting lists, the cross-city drives and your fears about quality of care, then, encouraged by strong ideologies about your rights to do so, you may have your children cared for from birth to adulthood by complete strangers at a cost. (Once at school they can have before- and after-school care, holiday care, and Saturday schools. You hardly need to see them!)

The second biggest decision a parent makes

The decision to have children is probably the biggest decision you ever make in your life. Deciding who will *raise* your children is the second biggest. We use the word 'raise' because the first five years are well-known to be the time of maximum intellectual and emotional growth. Children who go into care at two or three months of age, and stay for seven or eight hours a day, are basically spending their childhood in care. What kind of person they become – how they are comforted, how they are disciplined, what values and attitudes they will take on – will be the composite of the input of a large number of people, with widely varying styles and values. These children will certainly be adaptable! But will they be capable of intimacy? How will they integrate all these messages?

The two big questions – whether to have children, and who will care for them – are interlinked. As more than one crèche director has told us in private (after fighting off the pressure from parents to take younger and younger babies for longer and longer hours), 'I don't know why some of these people have children at all!' It's a fair comment.

The cuckoo culture

In the last ten years a kind of 'cuckoo culture' has developed. (Cuckoos are birds which lay their eggs in other birds' nests to be raised by them.) This trend has been encouraged through young women's magazines, and by media role models who portray this lifestyle as ideal. In some circles, having your kids raised for you is seen as a measure of success – the desirable norm.

We are a society that worships 'freedom', including freedom from the inconvenience of children. At the extreme end of the spectrum, there are sections of British society where children have become little more than a fashion accessory – window-dressing – wheeled out for a photo opportunity and then shuffled off to be attended to by others. It's fashionable to 'have' kids, but not necessarily to be encumbered by them.

We humans are very conformist creatures, and the perception that 'everyone does it' makes childcare as a choice seem harmless or even beneficial. So fashion, as much as real hard data, often influences these important decisions.

While the growth of this 'arm's length' parenting is a worry, the vast majority of parents are not like this. Most parents do want to raise their own children, do want the best for them, and are willing to sacrifice career aspirations and recreational or social goals to a high degree to achieve these aims. Increasingly men – even those in public life – are making decisions that favour parenthood over career.

Sadly, many parents feel forced by economic need to return to work when their children are young. They do so with immense regret. Others are confused, wanting to provide a nice home, toys, school fees, but not wanting to miss out on time with their children either. Whatever the reason, we need to know the real cost before making a decision.

A personal view

I had originally planned to write this chapter as an objective look at the childcare choices parents can make. It was the safe way – to sum up the arguments in what has been a long and worrying debate, and leave you to reach your own conclusions.

I soon realized, though, that to write in this way would have been wrong. I don't make my decisions as a parent by reading statistics or studies. I listen to these, but when it comes to the crunch I go on how I feel. Trusting intuition is what good parenting is all about. I'm guessing that you as a reader would prefer to hear my honest opinion, as opposed to pseudo-scientific fence-sitting.

I have strong concerns about childcare as it is used by many parents today, and believe that the damage it sometimes does to young children is of a hidden and long-term kind.

I am not alone. Professor Jay Belsky, probably the foremost academic in the field, argues that the evidence of damage is subtle; but it is enough that in 1986 he reversed his long-standing support for childcare for children under three. In early 1994, the world's foremost parenting author, Dr Penelope Leach, created a storm of concern by saying similar things, in her book *Children First*. I have always felt uneasy about the presence of babies and toddlers in creches. The more I have talked to people – parents, childcarers and adults who remember their own childhood experiences – the more my inner convictions have been strengthened.

I must stress that I cannot prove what I am about to say. The research hasn't been done yet, but like all parents I can't press a pause button on my children's lives until it's finished. All I can tell you is my point of view, so you can choose to agree, disagree or keep an open mind.

It is my belief that:

1. Long day care of children under three, in an institutional setting like a crèche, will result in those children having a seriously deprived childhood experience. The younger the children are when they enter childcare, and the longer the hours they spend there each day, the more serious will be their deprivation.
2. The problems and deficits will occur in many areas, but especially in those relating to emotional stability

intimacy and trust, and learning to develop lifelong relaxation and a peaceful inner world. This damage will be masked by an apparent gain in superficial social skills which actually reflect the child's strategies for coping with this stressful environment.

3. In the long-term, these deficits will lead especially to problems in forming and keeping long-term relationships. The general mental and physical health of these children is likely to be affected, and when they grow up they may have difficulty bonding with and caring for their own children.

In short, my belief is that, except in those cases of parents who are seriously impaired or genuinely incapable of raising their own children, young children are always better off being cared for by someone who loves them. Professionalism of staff and richness of surroundings, while important, don't touch on the question of love. Young children's bodies can be kept safe and their minds occupied, but their deeper, more subtle needs cannot be met except by someone with a fierce, long-term commitment to them. This is not something you can buy.

The plusses of childcare

The dangers of childcare suggested above have to be set alongside its benefits. It's clear to anyone associated with families:

- That all parents need breaks from the lonely and unnatural world of being at home alone with little children.

- That women have as much right as men to have and develop careers, and to be economically independent.

- That children in day care learn social and other skills, have enriched input and stimulation, and in many cases love and enjoy their time in crèches, family day care, or other childcare situations.

- That some parents are so ill equipped (materially or personally) that children are safer, happier and better off being cared for professionally for most of the time.

These plusses are well documented, and widely accepted.

Fearlessly facing the facts

The plusses are real, but so are the negatives. For a long time, however, the negatives have been suppressed – for fear of making parents feel guilty, or for fear of inviting even closer scrutiny and questioning of the childcare 'industry'. I think the first reason is patronizing, and the second is dishonest.

Childcare professionals often have a well-intentioned, but (I think) misplaced tendency to protect parents from concern. For example, there has been a long and important campaign by childcare academics and government centres in Australia to bring in national standards of childcare. This campaign was vigorously opposed by the private sector of the industry. A spokeswoman supporting better standards was quoted as saying, 'We didn't want to create hysteria by emphasizing cases where untrained fifteen-year-olds were left in charge of forty-five children.' The intention is admirable, but why should parents be seen as more hysterical than any other group? Parents care intensely about their children, and should be informed.

Is the rapid and widespread adoption of childcare a terrible thing? Or is it a wonderful breakthrough for parents – setting them free to have a better life? Is it a boon for children, given that many of us no longer live close to grandparents and relatives, who used to take this role, to have professionals to care for them (instead of amateurs like their mum and dad)? Or does it represent a serious loss of intimacy and specialness in childhood? Taking a middle road – can childcare be used in a balanced way to augment and enhance early childhood? However we view it, the childcare boom is a huge uncontrolled social experiment, and needs to be looked at with very clear eyes.

In this chapter we'll look at the reasons why people go back to work when their children are little, and whether these reasons are realistic. We'll discuss whether it actually makes more sense – and brings more joy – to stay home for a few years until your children are older.

Then we'll look at the realities of what care is available, so that when you do need it you can choose wisely. We'll examine what the hazards of childcare are so that you can analyse whether your child is suffering ill effects. We believe that once you are armed with this information you will be better able to make a choice that is right for you.

'But what if I have no choice?' – mothers who are forced to work

Many mothers with low-income-earning (or unemployed) partners, or single mothers, simply have no choice but to work, even though they would strongly prefer to be with their children. (This is a tragedy of national scale.)

My belief is that children can adapt to difficult circumstances if they understand the necessity. They can also intuit the truth. If your children know you would rather be with them, but that you have no choice, then the effect on their self-esteem is not nearly as severe as if they feel you just aren't interested in them – that you would rather be somewhere else.

Undermining the confidence of young parents

Sometimes young parents returning to work will argue that they are not 'good' at parenting – that their child would be better off with a carer. Yet it isn't as simple as being a good or bad parent – very few of us are good at it to begin with. Through the hours spent together, you become a good parent for that child. That's what a relationship (as opposed to a service) is all about.

Childcare can actually undermine your confidence. Sometimes parents feel that it makes the situation worse. They lose confidence and can be made to feel alienated from their child, not as loving nor as capable or interesting as the childcarer. The better others seem able to handle your baby or toddler, the lower your self-esteem sinks. It is more helpful to work with a parent – to give them skills, teach them more positive interactions and to care for them – rather than to bypass them and care for the baby. It's a sensitive question.

Stability and consistency, the underpinnings of a young child's world, seem impossible to attain in childcare. Even 'quality' care still means your child gets looked after by dozens of different individuals in the course of the four or so years before starting school. In reality, we cannot even organize the same location – a recent study found that some families had to access up to four different kinds of care in an average week to cover the hours they needed. Another study found great inconsistencies between centres, which children had to deal with in the round of a normal day.

Finding a balance that isn't a compromise

Life with toddlers in a lonely suburban house or flat can be a recipe for insanity if it is unrelieved by adult contact and activities other than housekeeping and parenting. So, for the wellbeing of adults and children, we need ways of providing safe care.

Friends, family day carers and childcare centres can all work well at different times of a child's life in different combinations to improve a family's life greatly. The key is to know what children's real needs are. This has been the missing piece in the discussion so far. Childcare was invented for the convenience of adults, not the needs or wishes of children. Those were an afterthought.

Research evidence, along with a revival of plain common sense, is leading to a reversal of the idea that a crèche childhood is a good childhood. I predict that there will be a definite move towards the use of childcare to augment parenting (rather than, as it is sometimes used today, as a virtual replacement for it). I also predict (and hope) that the use of childcare for babies and toddlers will be drastically reduced as parents realize the psychological and other costs.

We have left the 'you-can-have-it-all' 1980s, and are now in the 'get-real' 1990s. We are taking a fresh look at many things, and 'arm's length' childraising is one of them. People queueing for a childcare place may soon be met by a rush of people heading the other way.

News release

'Working mothers who send their young children to childcare centres may suffer from high levels of depression because of the separation, a new study has found. Some mothers lapsed into a depression serious enough to justify treatment by a psychiatrist, the study revealed.

'About eighty Melbourne mothers, who were putting their infants aged under two in suburban day care centres while working for financial needs, were interviewed by a University of Melbourne researcher. The study found that within the first two months of using childcare, many women complained of anxiety after being separated from their children. The anxiety sometimes led to depression. Four of the eighty women were suffering from severe clinical depression.

'About one in three of the working mums said they would have preferred to have stayed at home with their child instead of working and leaving their child in day care.'

('Working mums feel the pain of leaving children', *Mercury*, Hobart, 13 February 1993)

SEVEN SHAMELESS REASONS FOR STAYING HOME WHEN YOUR KIDS ARE SMALL!

1. **I'm selfish** – why should someone else enjoy my beautiful children while I slave away to pay for it? Why should they enjoy seeing them take their first steps, and come out with new words? Why should someone else get that glorious affection my children give out? I want it for me!
2. **I'm the best** – no one can raise my kids as well as I can. No one feels about them the way I do. No one knows them like I do.
3. **I'm supercautious** – I'm fastidious about safety, about guarding against abuse, about sensitivity to their feelings and what media they are exposed to. By being around all the time, I don't have to take chances on these issues – I know they are safe.
4. **I enjoy working in a team** – my partner and I work together well, we complement each other in parenting, and I like doing this with him or her. It's something else that makes us closer.
5. **I'm poor and proud** – I have so much self-esteem that I don't need great furniture or expensive clothes or a fancy house and car. I'm such a snob that I don't need money beyond the bare essentials. My kids are my jewellery.
6. **I'm lazy** – by raising secure and unhassled kids who feel safe and settled, I am making it easy for myself later on. I'm planning to cruise through their adolescence. And I'm teaching them fifty kinds of housework.
7. **I'm into it** – I enjoy the progress, the affection, the freedom to set my own pace, to decide how I will spend my time, the social get-togethers with other parents, the effect of the seasons on our activities, how my kids keep me young, and that I am (for this short time) the centre of their world.

Why parents choose childcare

There are four main reasons why parents return to work.

1. **Real financial need**
   Many families need both parents to be employed to survive. Many single mothers, too, need to work to provide adequately for their kids. For these families, childcare is a necessity of life. In one survey, 62 per cent of employed mothers indicated they would prefer to stay at home while children are below school age.

2. **Perceived financial need**
   Many couples feel that they need to work, but on closer examination this is based on a desire for a relatively high standard of living. As couples marry later and have children later, perhaps they have grown used to a high disposable income. A few decades ago, 'going without' was a normal part of life with young children and less of a concern. Our media images and expectations, and a competitive (rather than supportive) kind of society, mean that standards of income are much higher than actually required.

3. **Peer pressure**
   Many mothers feel they 'should' go to work, that this is the 'done thing', and that they are somehow defective if they 'just' want to raise children. Feminism has been ambiguous about motherhood, and the nurture of children has sometimes been devalued. For a man to prefer parenting to the full-time paid workforce is also seen as rather unusual.

4. **Enjoyment of career**
   Some mothers find their career so satisfying and enjoyable that it competes favourably with being at home with children. Sometimes their partner is more interested in full-time parenting, and so they reverse roles. At other times, neither partner is so keen on being with the children, and they place their children lower in their priorities.

Clearly, a multi-pronged approach is needed. We still need better-quality childcare, especially for the three to five age group where it is developmentally appropriate. We need the workplace to be much more family friendly, giving men and women parental leave, flexible hours, on-site childcare and 'sick child' leave. This will allow parents to make choices according to their own wisdom about what their family needs, and not be caught in impossible compromises.

If you do have a choice but just don't like parenting

The availability of childcare from babyhood has meant that many people decide to have children, while planning to have the bulk of their care done by others. Other parents feel that they are not really very good at parenting, and so it is better done by others.

But the fact is, many of us are not good parents to begin with. It comes with practice. Parenthood isn't a hobby, and it isn't a fair-weather kind of thing. There may be whole stages of the life cycle that you find very difficult – not all mothers like babies, some people find toddlers impossible, others dislike teenagers, and so on. Every parent at some time feels like giving up and retreating.

But there are usually reasons behind this that are worth getting to the bottom of.

It's in facing up to many crises and not giving in that we learn and really come to know ourselves and find how to be with children in a satisfying and happy way.

Is there a childcare syndrome? (How can I tell if childcare is harming my child?)

In the 1960s, there was some concern about whether institutional childcare harmed children. However, the research seemed reassuring – on the measures used, there was little if any difference. If anything, children in day care were more socially skilled, and somewhat more independent and assertive. Critics of these studies pointed out that almost all studies were of high quality centres, usually on university campuses convenient to the researchers, and far from representative of the real world.

So in the 1970s, the direction swung to investigating what was meant by 'quality', and whether this made a difference. It was found, not surprisingly, that smaller groups, better-educated carers, high staff ratios, all improved the outcomes. There was a risk identified of 'apathy and distress' among infants in larger groups, and 'boredom and tuning out' amongst older children if programmes were not well designed.

In the 1980s, researchers began to suspect that the kind of quality care parents want for their children might just not be possible in a formal setting. A secure, warm attachment to carers emerges again and again as the problem area. Gay Ochiltree, in summing up the research for her book, *Children in Australian Families* (Australian Institute of Family Studies 1992), points out the reality of high staff turnover in centres: 'The loss of an attachment figure can be very painful to a young child. When these observations are juxtaposed with the 40 per cent annual turnover among centre-based childcare providers and 60 per cent turnover among home based providers, there is tremendous cause for concern.'

In a penetrating and careful article, 'Infant Day Care, a Cause for Concern', Jay Belsky (who we mentioned earlier) analysed the entire body of research, collected from hundreds of studies from around the world in all imaginable conditions.

He found that there were suggestions of specific and recurrent damaging effects which emerged in many studies which, if not proven, were strongly indicated, especially when the research picture was looked at as a whole. In particular, he found four outcomes that were of concern in children who had entered childcare *before the age of one*:

- A pattern of withdrawal from and avoidance of the mother figure – babies and toddlers who did not approach their mothers, or see their mothers as sources of reassurance. The childcare experience seemed to make these little ones angry at their mothers, so that they did not turn to her for comfort. Their attachment was either displaced elsewhere, or they did not form strong attachments.

- Heightened aggressiveness – a tendency in the present, as well as later in school life, to use aggression, hitting, swearing, fighting, rather than talking through, walking away, staying calm.

- Non-compliance – ignoring or defying adults' requests or commands, doing the opposite, being rebellious.

- Social withdrawal – walking away, avoiding adult company, keeping to themselves.

These four effects were found across a wide range of studies – impoverished, middle class, upper class, in unstable family day care, high-quality centres, poor-quality centres, and even with at home babysitter care.

The effects are not surprising. Placed in the average childcare centre where other children compete for attention, where adult figures come and go, where the day is noisy and there is no private space, children learn to fend for themselves. They may learn not to place too much trust in adult figures, including their own mother, who is not there for them for much of the day. They cope as best they can, some probably better than others.

For parents, then, the question 'Is childcare harming my child?' can be answered with some clarity. If the child is regularly displaying a combination of the four symptoms listed above, then the answer is probably – 'Yes'.

'YOU CAN SPOT THE CHILDCARE KIDS'

While researching and interviewing parents for this section, we came across some revealing comments from parents who were also primary and infant school teachers.

'You can tell which kids have been in day care and crèches before starting school. They are really different.'

'It's hard to describe – they are kind of colder, less interested in you as a person. They can be quite good at manipulation.'

'Most little ones come along holding Mummy's hand – they are anxious, but they soon pass on the trust from their mother to you (the teacher). They are very affectionate and contactable. Childcare children seem kind of hardened – it's just another person, just another place. You often don't meet their parents either. They might have come from day care, and go back to it after school.'

'You get the impression these children have met lots of adults, and have no special feeling about it any more. They get on all right, get on with the day, but it's with a kind of resigned feeling. They are tougher, almost depressed.'

Comparing the options

There are many kinds of childcare options to choose from. Each has pluses and minuses. Let's look at each in turn so you can evaluate which, if any, are suited to your needs.

WHAT IS A DAYCARE CENTRE LIKE?

Most centres are purpose-built buildings about the size of a large house. They usually open from 8.00 a.m. to 6.00 p.m. or longer if they cater for parents who work shift work. They may offer full-time, part-time and occasional care. Regulations govern staff numbers, children's numbers, space indoors and out, toilets and so on.

Staff ratios are about one adult to five under two-year-olds, and one to fifteen over-twos. Some of the staff, but not all, need to have child-care or early childhood qualifications. Good centres will provide structured programmes similar to preschool activities so that children can learn through guided activity and play.

Fees vary from centre to centre but average about £95 per week. In some circumstances this is largely paid by government subsidy, in others it falls completely on the parents.

Childcare can be both expensive and cheap, depending on your point of view and your circumstances. The government estimates the average annual cost of full-time childcare is £5,200 per child, which is almost a fifth of the after-tax income of the average couple's (dual-income) full-time earnings. For some parents the cost (especially if you include petrol and, in many cases, the need for a second car) and the time involved, actually outweighs what they might earn.

A positive development is crèches provided by employers at the workplace. For giving child and parent easy access – at coffee breaks and lunchtime, for feeds, and in reducing travel time – this is a big improvement. Employers benefit too, from relaxed and happier staff.

REGISTERED CHILDMINDERS

This is a scheme by which local authorities license mothers in their own homes to care for up to five children from other families. Usually only one of these can be a baby; the others will be varied in age. Houses are inspected thoroughly for safety standards – child-safe cupboards, gates, fences and so on. Childminders' supervisors are watchful that good care is being provided, and will not license a childminder who is considered unsatisfactory.

When choosing a minder, the best bet is to look for someone who has been doing it for some time, and seems happy and well-organized. Trust your own feelings around that person, and about that household, and look carefully at the demeanour of the children there.

The huge plus is that childminders offer a home environment, and with luck can become a stable relationship where your child feels they are cared for as an individual. As with any trust relationship, time and getting to know a person are your only guides. If you are lucky, this person may become a family friend as well as a loving addition to your child's life.

Using a registered childminder is more personal than a childcare centre for you too. You can take the time to get to know your child's carer over a cuppa, and become friends as much as possible. It's fine to make a few enquiries and visit a few childminders to see how you 'click'. This is too important a relationship to leave to chance.

Because of the very low rates of pay to childminders for the responsible and skilled work they actually do, it is relatively cheap child care for parents. You can have a child with a childminder for a fifty-hour week for about £80–90 per week. Clearly registered childminders should be subsidized by government to make this an affordable alternative, and a worthwhile career path for carers.

There is a small but important risk in any childcare situation of sexual abuse, perhaps by a husband or older boy or girl in a household, or by workers or visitors at a centre. (Hospital studies have found that 10 per cent of serious abuse takes place in a childcare setting.) One criterion for letting your child be cared for by others is that the child has reached an age where they can tell you clearly if something is wrong.

NURSERY SCHOOLS

Nursery schools are exactly what the name suggests – a part-time introduction to school life for children aged around three to five. Many parents find them a great idea and decide when their child should begin depending on the individual child's readiness.

Nursery schools are a good childcare option for many parents. Since they are an outgrowth of school rather than of the need to have children minded, they are more educationally based than most other centres. Nursery schools usually run only a half-day or short-day session, and most children attend less than five days a week. (It's noteworthy that educationists consider this enough time for young children to be in a structured setting.)

Because of the short hours, nursery schools are ideal for at home parents, but are usually not convenient for employed parents who need longer hours.

NANNIES

Nannies are at-home one-to-one carers chosen and employed by you. This is obviously expensive, and quality is hugely variable. (Do they mind your child, or your TV set?) Nannying is a lonely job for someone who isn't really cut out for it. A caller to the Australian Broadcasting Corporation's *Offspring* programme told of her one-year-old son having three nannies in six months. 'Still,' she said, 'it's not much fun for seventeen-year-old girls being with a baby all day.' (Nor, we might add, is this situation much fun for the baby.) On the plus side, some nannies are superb, and an enormous help to the family unit. And the child is cared for in your home.

There is a side effect to nannies which most parents will be aware of, since it applies to any good-quality care. Studies of nanny use in affluent north American families found that a good nanny actually damaged the child's relationship with its mother, since the child naturally gravitated to the person who provided the warmth and time. It's an understandable problem, but it is really a problem of overuse which could be avoided by balancing time with mother, father and nanny. There is nothing wrong with loving lots of people.

FAMILY AND FRIENDS

By far the largest form of childcare used in Britain is still that provided by family and friends – grandparents, neighbours and so on. This is especially favoured by families of non-British origin, where family and cultural ties tend to be particularly strong and supportive.

When family and friends are caring for children, the same cautions still need to be observed and care must be taken that arrangements are fair to all concerned. But, by and large, children are loved and cared for because they are family, and this timeless way of sharing the joy and work of childrearing has a lot going for it.

DISCIPLINE – A PROBLEM AREA FOR CARERS

The pressure on a carer is to avoid trouble – to sidestep the discipline wrangles that parents at home with kids have to have, and from which children learn important lessons. Children who misbehave in care must be distracted, appeased, but not confronted (and we parents would not want carers to take such firm disciplinary action). It's the same with affection – it has to be diluted. Nap time is spent on a mat, not in an armchair in the arms of a loving relative. If carers wanted to give this amount of affection (and they often do) they would not have the time.

A child will often attract far more notice in childcare if they present a problem. Aggressive children, or very upset children, get attended to. Well-behaved children may be invisible. Childcarers have told us of the labelling syndrome, by which a child develops in the first few days an identity as a 'problem child', when it may just have been having a tough time settling in. The 'word' on who is being 'a problem' is passed on – from shift to shift and then from year to year. This reputation can follow a child right through to school.

A parent approaches their own child in a totally different way to the way they approach anyone else's. We talked to one crèche director who sends her own child to another crèche, because she felt it would be unfair to have him around when she is in her professional role. Another had the opposite policy – she wouldn't dream of having her child away from her.

We parents are intensely interested in our own child. Notice how you bore your friends with every detail of your child's progress. Look at it from the child's point of view. Might it not matter to a child to spend its first two or three years among people who adore it, who long to see it learn and grow, and have a personal investment and pride in it? Although a paid worker may genuinely care about children's wellbeing and advancement, the best they can ever feel is to be fond of your child, and be tender towards it in a general sort of way. What they have to offer will never equal a parent's investment and intensity.

QUALITY CARE IS STILL JUST CARE

The most overused word in the childcare debate is 'quality'. Nobody is happy with the idea of bleak, overcrowded childcare centres with cold and cruel staff. But 'quality' care is usually proposed as being equal to (or even, it is implied, better than) the care a parent can provide.

Care isn't love

The real question has to be whether children receive continuity of care, from individuals who have a long-term relationship with them, whom they come to trust and love.

Love is at the heart of the whole matter. It might be possible to improve the intimate connection children make with staff by addressing issues like staff rostering, size of groups, whether carers move through with the same group, and how many different adults are supposed to interact with a child during their time in care.

The debate about quality generally centres on training of staff, facilities, nutrition and educational programmes. All these are important, but they sidestep the question of quality relationships. Spending one's early childhood in the care of twenty or thirty different individuals (even in the best of settings) is still a very odd kind of childhood.

> The use of the word 'childcare' is a great piece of marketing. We have to ask: is childcare actually just 'minding' children, or 'educating' them, or is it 'raising' them? If you spend eight or nine hours a day of infancy and toddlerhood in a crèche, then these people are surely raising you. Yet no one in the childcare industry is proposing that professionals take over the primary role of the parents. It has somehow been assumed that parents will still provide all that is needed, even though parent–child contact time has shrunk, and shrunk, and shrunk. The development of intimacy skills in a child in care may not be happening at all. The child as a person may be falling through the cracks.
>
> Childcare academics have high aims, but the reality is often different. Childcare students and new workers we interviewed often spoke of the huge gap between their college or university ideals of 'individualized programmes' and 'one to one interaction', and the reality of life in a busy centre. Childcare is a highly stressed occupation – health problems, rapid turnover and total burnout in workers and directors are very common.

What is the big picture?

In order of preference, parents' first choice is family or close friends. The second choice – registered childminder – is also a more natural arrangement, where a mother at home cares for several other people's children, in a carefully regulated scheme that assures quality and safety. Childcare centres cater for the more mobile city-dwelling parents who need long day care beyond the ability of family or friends to provide, and need a more commercial arrangement.

Childcare can begin very young. It's not unusual for career parents in capital cities to place their babies in long day care at six or twelve weeks of age (sometimes from 7.30 a.m. to 6.00 p.m. for five days a week). Centre directors experience pressure to take babies at weekends too. Once these children reach school age, they will experience the daily two-step from home to before-school care, then school, then after-school care, then home.

Despite the demand, childcare is highly undervalued. Workers are abysmally underpaid. Many more mothers would choose to stay home with their own children and be registered childminders if the financial rewards were better. We just don't put enough value on children. In most British cities, it costs more to park your car than to park your kids.

The real problem – the motherhood ghetto

There are two things which drive mothers back to work when they would rather be at home.

One is economic dependency. Depending on another person's income can make the parent at home feel vulnerable and depressed. The non-earning partner can be made to feel that her work is worthless since she is 'just caring for kids'.

Another reason is the fear of 'going up the wall' – being with small children for company all day. This is a real problem, but not exactly a child's fault. The problem lies in the whole way we live. Our suburbs and apartment blocks may look pleasant enough, but are often very lonely places. We live surrounded by strangers, and the only social life is a trip to the supermarket. It's possible, through neighbourhood houses, playgroups, churches, swimming clubs and other organizations, to become more connected, and to bring about social change. But to do this, a person needs to be fairly confident and socially skilled.

It could be argued that Ethiopian farmers or Calcutta slum dwellers have a better life than Westerners in terms of social support and sheer friendliness of daily living.

Revitalizing the suburbs

If more parents were at home in the daytime, then things in the suburbs would soon change. You can already see this happening – playgroups, neighbourhood houses, and many other formal and informal networks of women and men are developing. Some of these will be oriented around children, others will be purely for self-development, or action groups for important issues like the environment, or more resources for families.

As men choose to be more family focused, and as more people work at home (thanks to computers) or work shorter hours, suburbs may change from deserted dormitories into lively and safer places where life goes on at its best.

Should parents be paid?

In many parts of the world, a radical idea is being discussed which has the potential to dramatically improve family life. The idea is that if we really value children, if we really want to 'save the family' we should pay a wage to mothers or fathers who choose to care for their own young children, full-time, at home.

Once, not long ago, families could live on the wage packet brought home by one person. The 1950s were not prosperous times, yet supporting a family was relatively easy. Today, fifty years later, many families need two incomes to survive. What has gone wrong ?

The two full-time income family is now very common, and often a necessity. But it is not a happy situation. In every street of every city and town in Britain, families are cracking up under the strain of both working and raising kids. You can see this amongst your friends, your neighbours, perhaps in your own house. Two-income families tell of horrendously stressed lifestyles, rushing to childcare each day, commuting across town, trying to snatch sleep each night, barely earning enough to offset the costs of childminding, transport and so on, then guiltily spending the money on making it up to the kids for not being there for them. Marriages are breaking down needlessly through sheer lack of time to build relationships. Health is being damaged through overwork, kids are being neglected and mistreated, and many teenagers are left to their own devices far too much. Serious problems, such as drug abuse, crime and early pregnancy, have all been found in studies to correlate with one reliable factor – lack of parental time and involvement.

It's not just our own kids. Parents used to give more time to running scout troops, helping at school, coaching children's sport, caring for elderly relatives: just being a community. Now it's all we can do to just make a living, feed the kids, get to sleep and go to work again the next day.

Is Life Just Earn and Spend?

The economic view of life that governments seem to have taken – whether New Labour or Old Conservative – is that we are here in this life to earn and spend. If you are not in a job, you are not a full member of society. Making Spice Girl dolls on a production line is seen as a valuable economic activity, but raising a child with care and skill is not. Yet the value of the work that is done at home is greater in real financial terms than all our mining, agriculture and manufacturing productivity put together.

I spoke about this to a Family Committee of MPs at the House of Commons in May 1998, and challenged the MPs present about whether they really valued parenting.

For instance, the Government has put a lot of pressure lately on single mothers to return to the workforce. This makes sense if they are not to be welfare dependent. But surely this could wait until their children are at least of school age. Several MPs tried to reassure me that they did not wish to devalue the role of mothers, but the reality, as some of the community representatives present pointed out, is that single mothers feel acutely insecure.

So the bottom line is this. Parents carry out an enormously valuable function. It just doesn't show up in financial terms except in a hidden way – ten years later, when we either have happy, healthy and contributing citizens, or rising crime, breakdown, misery and a horrific underclass that grows in size every year.

Millions of people don't have any work. And millions have too much work. Many people with jobs now work fifty- to sixty-hour weeks just to hold onto them. We should be smart enough to share work more, to flow flexibly between full- and part-time work, men and women swapping and sharing as our life cycle dictates.

The kind of economy we have now wants women, and not men. All through the eighties and nineties, jobs in manufacturing began disappearing, while demand for women in lowpaid service jobs soared. The result is a 'women's work ghetto' that tears young mothers in half as they try to balance children and income earning, in jobs which are often menial and boring.

The Right to Parent

Women and men have an equal right to work. But what about the right of mothers or fathers of young children NOT to work? At the moment, many women do not have this choice. (Working fathers have long been deprived of real time with their children.) Once women had to fight for the right to a career. It seems we now have to fight for the right to parent our own children.

How Would Parent Pay Work?

What would be the effect of paying a weekly grant to people who stay at home to raise their young children – say up to school age ?

The first thing would be to remove sexism. The choice of who goes to work and who stays at home should be an individual choice of the couple. A dad may well be the one who prefers to be the at-home parent. Stay-home fathers are a growing phenomenon worldwide.

A high proportion of mothers currently in full-time jobs (some studies put it around 60%) would prefer not to work while their children are very young, but cannot afford to stop working. A parent pay system would mean this group would begin vacating jobs, depending on the level of pay, and those jobs would be available to others currently unemployed.

This is not an argument for chaining women to the home. Both men and women need the stimulation, participation and rewards that work brings. However, going out to work must be a real choice. Women often have to work at unfulfilling, menial, deadend jobs while their little children are cared for by strangers at great expense, and with a lot of heartache, inconvenience and stress. (Sometimes they take these jobs because they are the only jobs that allow flexibility of hours.)

Some practicalities would be involved. Families would nominate who is the 'at home' parent, and that person would be personally entitled to parent pay. If they took part-time work, then parent pay would be reduced. To prevent dependency (or people having dozens of babies to cash in!) parent pay would NOT be based on the number of children. And it would cease once a child started school.

We can never actually reimburse the effort of parenthood. If carried out by paid professionals, parenting would cost over £50,000 per year per child. Yet even small grants to at home parents begin to make an impact, and it would be a matter of adjusting this amount to find where it began to make a difference.

Other countries have made moves in this direction. In Sweden the Government pays you 90% of your prebirth salary for up to 18 months from birth, for whichever parent leaves the workforce to care for the baby. Other countries use tax breaks and other means to help parents be parents.

Parent pay is very much a feminist cause. It's one of the most ingrained aspects of sexism to value the work of a male executive or a tycoon who might produce little of value, while devaluing the enormously positive work that is done in the home and the community by people (usually women) who are paid nothing.

Parent pay, even at a modest level, is a step towards a different kind of society, where the economy serves the people, and not the other way around. It is as fundamental and as powerful as that. Please think about it and talk it over with others. Sometimes we have to ask the big questions and get our society going in a better direction, and this is one of those times.

CONFLICTING VIEWS – THE EXPERTS SLUG IT OUT

'Poor quality care in these years can sometimes harm young children. Leaving babies and toddlers unattended and unoccupied for long periods, inappropriate discipline, lack of a good planned program or even leaving a distressed child uncomforted can make childcare an unhappy experience for parents and children alike.'

Labour Policy Statement, 1993 Federal election, Australia.

'I've never advised mothers who wanted a career not to pursue it, but I think it's very cruel for mothers who would rather stay at home to have to turn their kids over to someone else. If a mother wants to stay home with her baby, the Government should subsidise her, as in most other western countries.'

Benjamin Spock, the *Mercury*, Hobart, November 1992.

'From my experience, childcare (if carefully chosen) is not just good for children, they thrive on it! They benefit from a rich, stimulating environment away from the narrowness of an exclusive relationship with one parent. They have a larger view of the world and learn to share and cooperate with one another. They spend time with adults who enjoy being with them, and zoom in on their needs day after day. They are creative, self reliant and, I suspect, appreciate their parents a little more because their time together is so special.'

Rosemary Lever, *Such Sweet Sorrow.*

'Quality care is hard to come by, and even if you are one of the lucky ones, once your children are in care your life will entail a daily round of juggling childcare pickups and daily duties. If you're anything like me you will also have to live with a mixture of feelings and impossible contradictions, swinging between joy, happiness, or gloomy questioning about whether the care you have chosen is suitable, whether the children are happy, whether they're getting enough time and attention from you.'

Rosemary Lever, *Such Sweet Sorrow.*

'The fact is that the children of good, working parents are just as happy and turn out equally well as those of parents who don't work. It is not quantity of time you spend with your child that counts, it is the quality.'

Christopher Green, *Toddler Taming*.

'Regular absences can be damaging for children under three. Only from ages three to six, can most children profit from a whole day in high quality group care. But even then, there is a consensus among preschool educators that the benefits of a good preschool program diminish or are even cancelled when the school day is prolonged to six hours or beyond.'

Selma Fraiberg, child psychoanalyst, quoted by Karl Zinsmeister in 'Hard Truths about Day Care', *Readers Digest*, January 1989.

' . . . infants in day care are more likely to develop insecure attachments to their mothers, withdrawal from their mothers, and were more likely to hit, kick, threaten and argue, than those who were not in day care or started later.'

'Children with a record of early non-parental care show more serious aggression, less cooperation, less tolerance of frustration, more misbehaviour, and at times social withdrawal.'

Karl Zinsmeister, 'Hard Truths about Day Care', *Readers Digest*, January 1989.

' . . . the point is that day care was introduced for the adult's benefit and investigations into whether or not it is helpful or damaging for the child come later. Day care is about adult economics, adult behaviour, and adult desires.'

Bob Mullen, *Are Mothers Really Necessary?*

'Bruner (1980) concludes that in its present form, childminding creates problems for at least a third of the children in such care, and for possibly as many as half.'

Bob Mullen, *Are Mothers Really Necessary?*

'Sheila Kitzinger notes that the social context of childbearing has become negative and rejecting – childbearing is an interruption of people's "real" lives. Kirtzinger adds that this particular ethos which downgrades motherhood and childrearing, attributes to those mothers who find motherhood satisfying a mindless, sentimental form of idiocy. Kitzinger believes that in the women's movement, whatever that might be, there is an ambiguous approach to motherhood.'

Bob Mullen, *Are Mothers Really Necessary?*

'First time parents are often unprepared for the intensity of love they have for their children. One mother I met recently described it as being "metamorphosed". She held a senior position in a large banking firm and had committed herself whilst pregnant to an early return date. The day we met she marvelled about how changed she felt by the birth of her child, how privileged, how much more love she had to give and how painful it was even to contemplate leaving her precious baby with anyone else.'

Rosemary Lever, *Such Sweet Sorrow.*

Recommendations

The choices we make about childcare should be based firstly on the developmental needs of our child.

As mentioned earlier in this chapter, there are no conclusive research results that set down what is right for every child. We parents have to use our own good sense. The following are guidelines I recommend.

BY AGE

In your child's first year, do not use institutional childcare at all.

Organize for your baby to be with one of you all the time, except for occasional breaks – days off or evenings out, when you have a trusted and familiar babysitter.

If you are using institutional childcare, we suggest you consider these guidelines:

When the child is one – up to one short day per week, for example, 10 a.m. to 3 p.m.

When the child is two – up to two short days per week.

When the child is three – up to three short days or half-days a week.

When the child is four – up to four short days or half-days a week.

Your decisions should always be based on the needs of the individual child, and through monitoring its reactions from day to day.

BY TYPE OF CARE

In order of preference, we believe the best source of childcare for your child under the age of three would be:

✶✶✶ *Close relative or friend* whom you trust and who loves your child.

✶✶ A trustworthy and *friendly family day carer*, whom you know personally.*

✶ A *quality childcare centre*, with stable staff whom you get to know and feel comfortable with.

*If you cannot find a family day carer you are really comfortable with, then a childcare centre is probably better.

For children three years and older, good childcare centres can come into their own. At this age, the benefits of social interaction, planned activities, playing space and equipment, and professionally trained and motivated staff are a major bonus.

BY YOUR CIRCUMSTANCES

As well as the needs of the child, the needs of the family unit must be weighed in – because the child will suffer anyway if, for instance, a parent becomes sick, or a marriage breaks down, or a family cannot keep its home through lack of income.

If childcare is truly good for your family, it will be filling the following criteria:

1. It helps your survival – for instance, when you need to work to provide for material needs.

2. It gives you time to care adequately for other children, for example a new baby or a sick child.

3. It provides things for your child that you can't provide – resources (if poor), stimulation (if limited at home), friends (if isolated or an only child).

4. It meets your standards on discipline, respect for the child's being, and safety.

5. It builds long-term relationships – carers become your friends, and friends of your child.

6. It is a setting where you feel welcome to drop in at any time, spend the day with your child, make special requests or let them know of concerns, without ever feeling you are a bother.

By balancing a child's needs, and one's changing family situation, informed choices can be made which may work out very well.

Good luck!

Too, too, too

Childcare is here to stay. What we have to guard against is childcare overuse. Our standards have somehow slipped. We have been sucked in by economic rationalism, and stopped listening to our own hearts.

The result – children are being put into care too young, for too long hours, too many days a week.

The inadequate provision of childcare means that parents are having to use too many different forms of care, even in the same day, to meet their needs.

Childcare workers are paid too little, and there are too many children. Centre-based care is too unnatural and mechanistic a form of looking after young children, too factory-like for comfort.

In the future, there will be a place for childcare, but it will be a smaller place than it now occupies. While everyone talks about the need for more childcare places and bemoans the waiting lists, it may be that one day there will be less demand for it, and places will be abundant for those who really need it. Little babies and toddlers will mainly be cared for once again where they have been for millennia – by their parents, neighbours and family members, in the arms and in the homes of those who love them.

IS THIS THE PERFECT WAY TO LIVE?

On a wooded suburban ridge overlooking Hobart's harbour, a cluster of houses stands out only slightly from the conventional houses close by. They have warm, earthy colours, detailed woodwork in Tasmanian timbers. More noticeably, they have no road, only landscaped pathways and discreet parking bays at the edge of the three-acre site.

This is the Cascade Cohouse – a form of living for people of all ages that has been highly successful in northern Europe, and is now gaining a foothold in Australia. For a young family that has to live in the city, this may well be the perfect way to live.

The setup

Cascade Cohouse consists of fifteen dwellings which run along a hillside, curving at one end to face a larger common building which everyone shares the use of.

A large, attractive 'village square' is at the centre and a pedestrian pathway curves amidst gardens and terraces. On completion of the Cohouse, thirty to forty people will live here. They will each own their own freehold. Each dwelling fronts on to common pedestrian space, but has a private back garden.

Best of all, all occupants will share in the large common building with dining room for forty people, children's playroom, well-equipped workshop, meditation spaces, office space and kitchens. Occupants may interact and join with other people on a daily basis, or be entirely private since the houses are quite self-contained.

This isn't a commune yet it is a real community. One of the nicest parts of Cohouse living is that a shared evening meal system exists. Each adult member is rostered to cook a meal for the community from time to time. At present that means once every eight weeks – it's your turn! Eventually these meals will be held four evenings a week. For a young working father or mother, this means that instead of arriving home from work and scraping a meal together for the family, one can often simply stroll over to the Commonhouse for a delicious prepared dinner.

A safe place for children to grow

Ian and Jane, two young scientists who were founding members of the Cohouse, explained how the Cohouse situation was ideal for them as parents of a two-year-old child. They could, if they wished, go out two or three nights a week and have excellent childminding available. Their little girl could walk to the houses of her young friends or older members of the Cohouse who enjoyed having young ones around. Since this was a group of people who knew each other and chose to live in community, the feeling of trust and companionship was everywhere.

Young mothers or fathers at home during the day had company for a chat simply by strolling outside or going to the Commonhouse. There was a flat for visitors of residents.

Older people felt secure and never lonely – although privacy was respected and designed into the buildings.

Inexpensive living

Costwise, the residents at Cascade Cohouse found that they could build a very attractive dwelling of ten to twelve squares for around £35,000. Purchasing the freehold and common ownership of facilities – including the thirty square Commonhouse – cost an additional £16,000 or so. This included all hidden costs such as service connection and stamp duty (which normally add over £4,000 to the cost of a suburban block).

Cohouses provide many qualities in living that simply could not be bought – companionship, safety, meals, low travel costs, solar design and all kinds of sharing potential. Some cohouses in Europe have shared ownership in holiday homes and yachts at the coast, and have their own swimming pool or sauna.

5

Raising boys

**It's time that we plan
for a new kind of man ...**

If you have a daughter, then things are looking up for her. Because of the gains women have struggled for and won in the last few decades, your daughter will have as much chance of being a doctor as of being a nurse, a boss as a secretary. She will have the right to equal pay, the right to leave a violent husband, and the means to do so. Nobody will own her.

But there is still a long way to go. Your daughter will not have the freedom to walk about at night. In her life she will meet all kinds of barriers caused by men's inner insecurities. She may have trouble finding a man to settle down with who is as emotionally healthy as she is. Clearly, in the progress we are making through feminism, there's a missing step – something has still got to happen with *men* to bring them along on the journey to freedom that women are making. We can make a big difference if we start early, with boys.

Giving boys a positive self-image

Think about the present situation of boys. If you hear on the radio about a gang of youths causing a fight, you're pretty sure it will be boys, not girls. When we talk about teenage suicide, in four out of five cases we mean boys. The driver of a crashed car, the cause of a high-speed chase, the problem child in the classroom or playground, the burglar, the serial killer, the corporate criminal, the dictator – why is it almost always a bloke?

> Boys have five times as many learning problems, ten times as much problem behaviour at school. As adults they will have four times the vehicle accident rate, and nine times the imprisonment rate.

If you have boy children, it isn't enough to let them grow up to be 'normal' – because normal for a man in today's world often means uptight, competitive and emotionally illiterate. It's time to start raising a 'new kind of man'.

This chapter is about realizing just how much more we can expect of boys if we are willing to expand our horizons for them.

The first step for us as parents is to get a clear idea of the kind of men we want our sons to be.

WHAT KIND OF MAN DO WE NEED?

A group of women is meeting in a weekend seminar on relationships. (In another room, the men who are their partners are also meeting together.) The leader asks the women to call out the qualities they look for in a man. After the quick rush of jokes, like 'Lots of money', and some unprintable comments, the women become more thoughtful. This is the list that they come up with.

Passionate

Self-reliant

Willing to share the work

Able to love deeply

Able to feel sorrow and admit fear, and not just turn everything into anger

Respectful to and supportive of women

Nurturing

Fearless and strong in good causes

Creative – not rigid or bound by convention

Respectful of others

Funny, but knows when to be serious

Stable, reliable (but not dull)

Sticks to a task, gets things done

Loving, but not gooey or dependent

Proud, but not egotistical

Safe and not violent

Able to dance and sing and enjoy the flowers

Not just a workaholic

Wild and free

Impulsive

Natural

These are what women look for in a man. It's a fairly safe bet that these are also what men are wanting to be in themselves.

So, when we are raising our sons, these can be some of the aims we have in mind. This awareness will guide our actions and help us know when to intervene in the smallest of everyday situations. When a boy is mean to his sister, or tickles her when she is clearly saying no – then as parents we come in very firmly and tell him not to do that. We would do just the same if she was mean to him. If he asks why, we tell him, 'I want you to grow up respecting people's bodies, and respecting your own too. When someone says *stop*, you *stop*.' You can see how important this is for a lifetime.

How the world treats boys

There's something special and precious about boys – every parent of boys and girls notices that their natures are different. Boys tend to wear their feelings on their sleeves – often their passions are strong and they seem to have an urge to protect. They love heroism and action. Boys are loyal, stoic, and have a strong sense of justice. They are humorous, optimistic and up-front.

When I look at little boys, and then see how cheaply the world often treats them – how few of their special qualities are supported and nurtured – it makes me very sad.

There are two facts that sum up the situation of boys, and how much needs to be done to help them. First, the news released by UNICEF that Australia has the highest rate of youth suicide of any Western country, and that suicide is four times more common among our teenage boys than girls. The second is a figure reported some years ago – that fathers on average spend six minutes a day in interaction with their sons. Neither of these is much to be proud of, and the two are very probably linked. So it's timely that we look at what we can do to help boys turn out well.

We'll sum up what is needed, then go into each issue more fully.

1. Boys need fathers, or at least very good father-substitutes.

2. Fathers need help from other men to raise their sons.

3. Boys need to learn how to behave around girls – respecting them, being equal to them.

4. Boys need protection from being cheapened, hardened or debased by exposure to violence or banality. They need to see their sexuality as special, not cheap.

5. Boys need help to learn how to work and be self-sufficient around the house.

Where have all the fathers gone?

One hundred and fifty years ago, life was very different for men and boys. Almost all men worked in agriculture and home-based crafts and trades. So a boy grew up around his dad and the other men of the village or town; his uncles, cousins, grandparents, all took an interest in teaching him and befriending him. Then suddenly, when the industrial revolution began, whole villages were evicted and millions of people went to the cities and towns to work in the mills and mines. Mothers had the task of raising their sons, as the fathers were away at work six days a week for long hours. 'Wait till your father gets home!' became a common catchcry.

Losing the support of the village network, the family itself started to decline. A hundred years ago, an average family had 6.7 children. Few people we know want to go back to that! But families didn't just get smaller. They started to fall apart. Men left their wives, or never married in the first place. Soon a large number of children were being raised by single women. This trend has continued to the present day. Men are disappearing from the family picture. For instance, within a year of divorce, one-third of fathers have virtually disappeared from their children's lives.

A father can be around and still have 'disappeared' emotionally. Many working men are out of the home early, home late, and tired and ratty when they are at home. Little children may not see their father at all during the week – they are asleep when he leaves in the morning and again when he comes home at night. An unemployed father, if he gets his act together, has a better chance of being a good father than someone with a busy career.

Father absence hurts and damages little girls too, but it devastates little boys. Whether they show it by being aggressive, or compensate by being Mummy's little helper, a boy with no role models cannot learn how to be a man. Some psychologists believe it may take hours a day of male contact for a boy to learn how to be a man. If little David has a lady schoolteacher, lives with his mum, stays at Grandma's, and meets only Mum's women friends at home, he learns nothing about how to be a man. The absence of men in boys' lives is a big problem in our society.

What can you do if you're a single mum?

Women on their own can raise healthy sons. But, as I've learned from talking to lots of single mothers, it takes some special planning.

BEING FIRM, STAYING WARM

A single parent of either sex continually has to switch between and balance the firmlove and softlove sides of their nature. For a single mother, there will be a danger of losing the softness while trying to maintain the firmness you know your son needs. As a rule, women are less combative than men in their interaction style. You can see this in the way some men say things like, 'Not you again!', 'G'day you old bastard' and so on in their friendly greetings. So discipline generally comes more easily for a father than a mother. In fact, sometimes while a mother is trying to be firmer, her partner is trying to tone down his hardness and be more reasonable.

There are times when boys (mostly unconsciously) seek out a combative (friendly, safe, but very confronting) intensity to help them deal with their physical and hormonal surges. Get help – from friends, or professionally – if you feel you are losing the plot here. Especially with boys around fourteen years of age, a mother on her own needs to conserve energy and be well supported. It's especially important never to hit or strike out, or say hurtful kinds of things at these times.

FINDING THE RIGHT ROLE MODELS

You must actively look for role models for your son. Go down to the school and ask the headteacher for a good male teacher for your son next year. When choosing a sport or activity, choose it by looking at the kind of men that lead the activity. Is this the kind of man I want my son to be like? (That is what role model means. Looked at this way, the football coach or karate teacher could be great, or the pits!)

Sometimes an uncle or grandfather will take an interest if you ask them to do so – they may have been holding back because they were unsure if their help was welcome. You don't have to marry someone to get a good role model.

Be very, very choosy who your son spends time with. Paedophiles (men who sexually abuse children) often take advantage of boys with no fathers who are hungry for male attention. This isn't a rare problem – one in seven boys is abused at some time in his childhood. Always check out the men in your son's life.

SEND HIM TO HIS DAD

Unless your son's father is a dangerous or very irresponsible man, do your best to maintain contact between them. If you are separated or divorced,

WHY BOYS PLAY UP

Marcus is fourteen. He likes to go off in the evenings on his bike and muck around with his mates. One night, he's late for tea. When he comes in, his parents grumble and nag at him, but his father is only half-hearted about it. In the end, it's agreed that Marcus can come in when he pleases as long as he's in by dark, and that his tea will be left in the oven.

A few weeks later Marcus comes in really late, about nine o'clock. He says it wasn't really dark. His mother is upset, but his father says, 'Well, as long as he doesn't get into any serious trouble, and is in by ten. Boys like to have a bit of freedom.'

A few days later, Marcus is brought home by the police, who found him with CDs stolen from a nearby shopping centre. He is one of a group of mates to be charged with the offence.

Marcus's parents, especially his father, wanted to avoid trouble. But they missed the point that Marcus was breaking the rules to get noticed. When the rules were just bent to give him more scope, he had to break even bigger rules. Marcus's father is a senior manager, and has been away overseas a lot. An intelligent man, he will now make the connection and start to do some fathering. Marcus will be confronted about his behaviour, but, more importantly, his father will get more involved. A promotion involving extra travel will be knocked back so that he can be at home more of the time. It will cost him materially, but Marcus will stay out of jail.

Boys play up because they want to be 'met' by an equal investment of energy, preferably from fathers or father-substitutes. Boys whose fathers are uninvolved are especially drawn to 'hypermasculine' action figures, comics and games. They are trying to make up for the lack of masculinity in their real lives. Boys with involved fathers are noticeably quieter, more communicative and more settled. They achieve more at school, have fewer behaviour problems and are more often employed when they leave school.

Studies have found the incidence of drug addiction and alcoholism in boys is directly proportionate to the amount of time spent with parents. Adolescence is not a time to ignore your children.

but in good communication with your ex-husband, consider sending your son to live with his dad from the time the boy is about fourteen years old. Often boys get difficult to manage around fourteen. Without realizing it, they feel a strong need for male limit-setting. Women often fear taking this step – 'Oh, he wouldn't look after him properly!' Sometimes this is true. But more often fathers, if called upon to take on the parenting, will find that they have untapped nurturing and disciplining qualities. This arrangement can work out well for everyone.

Single parenting is heroic work. It's better to be a child in a single-parent home than in a bitterly unhappy intact family. The challenge for single parents is to supplement your own parenting with the right inputs for your kids.

What fathering really means

Many dads are great with their kids. However, many of us are completely at a loss regarding 'how to father'. Early in my children's lives I found it tempting to just leave parenting to my wife because she seemed so much better at it. Today, though, fathering is one of the biggest pleasures of my life.

Part of the reason for our incompetence is that we have a fathering vacuum – many men didn't have an involved father, just a strange man who shuffled newspapers in the corner of the lounge and grumbled occasionally. So we didn't have a deep pool of fathering behaviours to draw from.

Luckily I can say to you from experience, 'It ain't that hard' and 'Once you get started you'll soon get to like it.' Here are two or three good ways to start.

ROUGH AND TUMBLE

Boys love to wrestle, tickle, struggle, and play in vigorous, rough and tumble ways. This seems to be true at any age. Do this whenever you get the chance and have the energy. Choose a safe place. Give them a goal – to pin your arms, or escape from a bear hug.

There is more to it than just good fun – you can teach important lessons while you wrestle. By stopping if it gets too careless or dangerous, calming down and beginning again, you are teaching boys to handle and be calm with their strength. By always being good-humoured and not excessively competitive – letting them win, then winning again – you teach them that the fun is in the interaction, and to be good losers. Perhaps most importantly, play wrestling or 'rough and tough' is both a form of intimacy and a celebration of masculinity. (Though some daughters like it too, especially when they are little.)

My own father was not into hugging or outward displays of affection and, like many men of his generation, couldn't give a compliment to save his life. But he would always play wrestle with me, with my cousins and with nephews. Whenever we went visiting, he would be covered with kids. It was great!

DOING AND TEACHING

Robert Bly says, 'Even mean men are sweet when they teach.' Boys love to learn about the world of men. This might mean cars, computers, horses, birdwatching, football, fishing, woodwork – anything that they enjoy, and you enjoy showing them. (A clue – don't be perfectionist, or you'll just put them off. Share your enjoyment, not just your high standards.)

If you're a dad, you should be around your son and the rest of the family, talking and doing things, for at least an hour a day. If your work schedule prevents this, you might need to look seriously at your priorities. I would like to be more comforting about this, but being a career success today is almost incompatible with being a good father. Boys need to know you in all different moods and different activities.

SEEING YOU IN ACTION

If sons see you cooking meals, cleaning up and caring for younger kids, then they will also become more hard working around the home. Dads have to show they are more than just 'the good times man'. You can teach them by example how to be whole men. If they see you taking care of your body, treating other people well, expressing your emotions, standing up for what you believe in, then this will be more powerful than anything you might say. You might just have to become the kind of man you want your sons to be!

LISTEN UP!

One of the greatest life skills you can ever have is the ability – the willingness, really – to stop in the middle of an argument and listen to the other person's side of the story. It's a skill you could use at least five times a day . . .

One hot summer afternoon my son and I went down the gully to start the diesel pump. We do this once every summer to refill our dam with water. My son was four – a little young, you might say, but a necessary assistant. While I cranked the pump, his job was to flick the pressure switch at the critical moment for the pump to start.

The machine is huge and old, and we had several failed attempts. I was not in a good mood. Thistles stung my legs, and mosquitoes swirled about. My arm ached from turning the heavy crank. Then my assistant went on strike! He backed off around the dam! I could feel my anger rise. I prepared myself to bully him into doing as he was told. But he looked me squarely in the eyes, accusing almost, and I managed to catch myself. 'Why won't you help?' I asked, trying to make my voice sympathetic. 'It's too smoky. I can't breathe,' he said. Sure enough, a pall of diesel fumes hung around from our first attempts.

So we sat by the water for a few minutes, quietly relaxing before trying again. We chatted a little about the frogs and the insects. Then we started the pump first time!

It hasn't been the last time, and probably the experience gets more frequent as children get older and wiser. That moment of simple parental realization – 'They're right and I'm wrong.' And how important it is to listen.

LET YOUR SON MEET OTHER MEN

Involve your sons in activities with your friends so they can meet, learn from and get the approval of other men. Go on fathers-and-sons camping trips. Take your sons to work so that they see from time to time what you do with your life – where you fit into the big picture, what your ideals are. Let them see some of what you sacrifice, some of the hardship and endurance that your life involves.

Above all, be around for them. Have time to waste.

Boys need protection

I was once waiting outside a primary school for a meeting at the end of the school day. A group of boys – grade three, eight-year-olds – were coming slowly out of the classroom. Seeing something wasn't quite right, I looked more closely. Several were wiping tears from their eyes. All looked pale, shocked. I discovered later from a parent that their teacher – a man – had just shown an '18' rated war video because it was Armistice Day. No discussion, no debriefing, no breaks – just ninety minutes of violence. Often men and boys get blamed for being unfeeling, aggressive, insensitive. But how do they become that way, except as a defence against what we assail them with?

You can do a lot to slow down the robbing of childhood from your sons (and daughters) by preventing them from watching endless violent cartoons or playing unimaginative games with war toys. (Kids do make guns from sticks, yes, but all you can do with a toy gun is pretend to kill.) Much war and violent play arises from watching violence, feeling frightened by it and so identifying with the war figures to get back a sense of power. Children in war zones play the most war games. Why should our sitting rooms resemble war zones? Why not have a home (and a TV environment) that brings in the feeling of a tropical island paradise, with nature, warmth, beauty and adventure?

It's the same with computers. Don't let your sons 'disappear' into banal computer games for hours on end – especially the kind with endless mazes and ladders – which are addictive and teach nothing but a twitchy finger.

Provide more active, sociable and natural kinds of activity. Spend time with your sons rather than buying things for them. Value and compliment their ability with little children, and their sensitivity to feelings and fairness. Have a pet that they can be active with. Do this and you will see the natural lovingness come out in your boys.

Boys need help in learning to relate

One good thing that a mother or father of boys can do is to teach them to get along with the opposite sex, and help them to talk to and cooperate with girls. Insist they treat girls with respect and care. When they become teenagers, don't let them put pictures from girlie magazines on their walls. Most boys are interested in women's bodies, but you can help to keep sex and sexuality special and not just sleazy and cheap.

Teach your son to respect women

As a dad, you do this in two ways – by showing respect to women yourself, and by coming down hard on any disrespect that is shown by a son to his mother. An old saying, 'Don't speak to your mother like that', sets the scene for an important moment in family life. It should only need to be said once.

As a mum, calmly and clearly demand respect. Mediate with your son and his sisters so that they are able to express their feelings, and to learn respectful problem-solving instead of name-calling and intimidation. Be even-handed. Boys have feelings – remember this yourself, and teach your daughters this. If boys are treated as though they have no feelings, then they become unfeeling to protect themselves.

Ask your son about his feelings and acknowledge when he is sad or scared. Let him know when you have these feelings too. Avoid the emotional shutdown that makes men so stressed and depressed. Don't ever make fun of his soft side, especially his early love life. He can be strong and sensitive. They go together.

Help him learn housework skills

And praise those skills! By age nine, a son should be cooking a meal for the family each week and feeling proud of it. Even if it's only pasta and ready-made sauce to begin with, he can soon build up a creditable menu. Help him to get started in the kitchen. Most boys will gain enjoyment from making such a contribution.

Make it routine that he picks up after himself, learns to do laundry and to mend. If he doesn't, don't nag – just double his workload for that day. The common response from Supermum types is, 'But it's quicker if I do it for him – he just takes so long.' Yes, teaching takes time. But imagine having an eighteen-year-old who is as competent as you are, and who does as much housework as you do. Surely that's worth a little early investment!

In short

You are making a man. Think about the goals you have achieved, and those you still want to achieve. You could tick off on the list given by the women in the class at the start of this chapter (page 251). Which do you still want to work on?

At the very least, take time to have a dream about the kind of man you want your son to be. By making a commitment – 'My sons will turn into wonderful young men' – and starting to do the daily things that make this happen, you can, as a mother or father, achieve one of life's greatest satisfactions, and do the world a favour.

6

Raising daughters

Through her daughter, a mother sees her own life starting again. So a daughter has a powerful effect on her mother. And how a mother feels about her own life will deeply influence how she relates to her daughter.

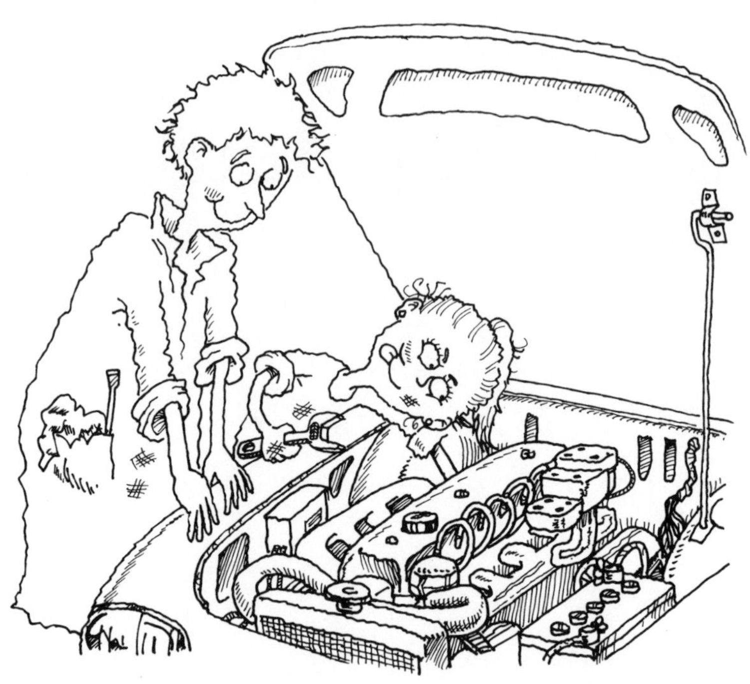

Mothers and daughters Mothers and daughters can have a closeness that is very beautiful. Or they can be an explosive combination! Mums and daughters usually understand each other deeply – sometimes to an extent that seems telepathic.

Mothers feel so strongly about their daughters, just as fathers do about their sons, because in a sense our children are a new version of us. They reflect back to us all our hopes, fears and feelings about our own lives. If you know this is going on, it helps. If you don't, it can lead to very weird behaviour! Things can get fiery, as our teenagers become especially sensitive to being loaded up with our expectations. Such situations have led more than one mother to tell me she prefers sons – they're so much simpler!

But it's worth it. Part of what makes raising a daughter so great an adventure for a mother is the potential for close friendship. In the meantime, though, your daughter is a little child needing your care. To care for her well, you may have to work free of some of your own hang-ups that could be getting in the way of clear parenting.

What do we mean by this? Let's expand.

Mothers see themselves in their daughters. For better or for worse, this generates all kinds of unconscious and conscious urges.

- They want their daughters to have more opportunities than they had.
- They want their daughters to stay close, but also to move out and have their own life.
- They want their daughters to get on with their dads.
- They want their daughters to find a man – as long as he's perfect!
- They want their daughters to have a life free from pain or trouble of any kind.

What do we mean by unconscious urges? Here's an example: A friend of mine had a mother who had known great poverty in her childhood. Her idea of good mothering was working long hours so that her daughters would be well provided for. The result was that her daughters had very little time with her, and were often placed in vulnerable situations while their mother was away at work. They would have been better off with less money and more protection.

Sometimes when our motivation is unconscious like this, we don't think through all the ramifications. The key to this is self-awareness. You listen to what comes out of your own mouth, and reflect on 'where you are coming from'. You realize that your daughters are not you, and give them room to make their own mistakes, find their own answers, define what they want.

The five ways of parenting

Jean Illsley Clarke, in a superb book called *Growing up Again*, describes five different ways we can react to a child, which also tell us a great deal about ourselves. You can use these five styles as a diagnostic tool to find what is happening between you and your daughter. Most probably, you'll find confirmation that you are doing the right thing, which Clarke calls the 'assertively caring' style. The other styles can easily be recognized and help you to avoid doing harm.

When I first learned about these ideas (and this is talking as a dad) I found I was a real mixture of the different types. It was very helpful to think about.

Let's apply the five styles to a simple everyday situation: Merrilee, a little girl aged six, falls over while running in the park. She comes to her mother crying, with a badly scraped arm.

There are several ways her mother can react.

THE ABUSIVE STYLE

Her mother is busy talking to a friend. She turns and yells, 'Stop howling like that, or I'll really give you something to cry about.' As she does so, she yanks the little girl by the arm and takes her off home.

The message sent here is, 'You don't count. Your feelings don't matter. You're a nuisance to me.'

The child may feel deep pain and despair, or rage, or loneliness and withdrawal. But where is the mum coming from? If we're honest, many of us have felt overwhelmed at times, and reacted in a verbally abusive way. It's the reaction of a parent whose own needs are so unmet that she sees her daughter as a competitor.

This mother needs help of a nurturing, long-term kind so that she can refill her emotional fuel tank, heal her own childhood neglect, and in the meantime care for her daughter with more kindness.

THE CONDITIONAL STYLE

This mother says, 'Stop crying or I won't bandage your arm. What did you do that for anyway?' This kind of parent connects with the child by threats and conditions. The child has to meet with parental expectations, and only then will her needs be met. The message is, 'Don't believe you are loveable, you only get love if you earn it.'

The mother sends this message to her daughter because it's how she also views herself. This kind of parent is usually immaculate and uptight, setting super-high standards for herself and those around her. It's natural she will pass on the same messages to her child – especially if the child is the same sex child as herself.

The child will feel inadequate, never quite measuring up – since no one is ever perfect. The child is likely to grow up obsessive and over-achieving, perhaps anorexic, with a lot of trouble being close to other people. In adulthood, she may have a series of showy but short-lived marriages.

The conditional Mum needs to relax. She has to learn to find – and to give herself – love and approval just for being. She can learn to stop worrying so much about clothes, looks, money or achievement. She should find some friends who are happy slobs, and learn how it's done. In this way she can learn to accept that love is free and doesn't have to be earned. And then she can teach this to her children.

THE INDULGENT STYLE

Mummy rushes to the child before the little one has even had time to stand up. 'Oh, look at your arm. That really hurts, doesn't it? I'll bandage it now. We'll drive to the chemist and get some ointment. I'll make you a bed on the couch in front of the TV and I'll do your jobs for you.'

This sounds at first like a very kind mother. But listen to the deeper messages: 'You are a poor victim. You aren't capable – you need me to look after you.' At an even deeper level she is implying, 'We can't both meet our needs at the one time. I'll overindulge you, but you'll owe me.' Does this sound familiar to you?

The child in this relationship will have very mixed feelings. She will feel temporary comfort, but also a sense of obligation and resentment underlying it. She will feel weakened and confused by her parent's presence, rather than strengthened and encouraged. Jean Illsley Clarke calls this 'a sticky, patronising kind of love' which promotes dependency and a blurry sense of self.

The mother in this situation needs to build a stronger sense of self. Perhaps her childhood featured an alcoholic or otherwise needy parent who forced her to grow up too soon, and to be a caretaker instead of being loved. Perhaps one of her parents was also indulgent to mask inner neediness. She could benefit from reading books about codependency and getting good support in a healing kind of ongoing group.

THE NEGLECTFUL STYLE

Mum ignores the scrape. In fact, she's probably not even at the playground. The daughter is far from home, unsupervised, and nobody cares. This child may be fed and clothed, but her parents are uninvolved. She knows deep down that she dies or survives alone. If she has made it this far she will probably survive, but she is likely to be a very hard, lonely young person with all kinds of anger and disappointment hidden on the inside. She will possibly get into serious strife in an attempt to get cared for. As an adult she will have little ability to get close to others, unless help – in the form of an understanding teacher or youth worker – comes along soon.

Neglect is abuse, too – in some ways, one of the worst forms.

Before you get totally depressed, we'd better talk about the fifth kind of parenting style.

THE ASSERTIVELY CARING STYLE

This mother gives the little girl with the scraped arm a hug and loving care. She says things like, 'Your arm is scraped. I'm sorry you are hurt. How about I clean it up for you?' And then, 'How is it now?'

The child knows that she and her feelings matter. The mother is willing and available to help. Help is offered, not forced. The child feels comforted and relieved, secure, safe and loved.

There's more, too, in the big picture. This kind of mother lets her child grow in independence. If the child is only slightly hurt, or is somewhat older, the mother leaves her in charge of what happens. She says things like, 'Does it hurt? Are you able to go and wash it, or do you need some help?' This parent is available to give a hug, but is not too pushy. The message sent here is – 'I trust you to make your own judgements about what you need' (and, also, 'I don't need to be needed').

The assertively caring style is clearly the one to aim for.

Fathers with daughters

One of the things I've been struck by in my work is the great importance of fathers in shaping their daughters' self-esteem. I especially believe fathers should never put down their daughters' appearance even in 'fun'. Some men do this, perhaps out of some motive to 'tidy them up' or make them more presentable. The effect is usually the complete reverse.

There are many good things dads can do. They can give praise. They can also enjoy joking and laughing with their daughters, developing their skills in conversation and repartee. Be alert to the fact that girls change and go through very different phases, so that what was once a good topic to joke about can become an acutely sensitive one which is better left alone.

Fathers are a source of opposite-sex social practice. By conversing with their fathers about serious issues, by being admired for their mind as much as for their looks, girls learn to approach the opposite sex with the skills necessary to take the initiative and give as good as they get. They will never be bluffed or intimidated in male company. They will also have the confidence to pick and choose their partner rather than being passive wallflowers.

Building self-reliance in girls

A father can build some good independence skills with his daughter – teaching her about cars, fixing things, woodworking, dealing with money, going camping. In this way he'll know she's safer out in the real world, and less dependent.

In a recent article, comedian Jean Kittson told how she grew up in a town where 'boys had cars, and girls had boyfriends'. She decided to get a car instead of a boyfriend, with her father's help, and escaped to the big smoke and a great career instead of being someone else's ornament!

Close but safe

Fathers who are clear about not sexually invading their daughters can still be affectionate and warm – they don't have to get all uptight. Sexual touch and affectionate touch are totally distinct.

Having a strong marriage also helps your daughter's development – she sees a man and woman relating respectfully. If a daughter knows that her parents are close, then she will feel safer around her father, since his needs for affection and sexual partnership are clearly being met. For this reason, be wary of taking your daughter's side against your partner – if you have a problem with your partner, then deal with it on a one-to-one basis.

Respect is a key element between the genders and you as a father can model it. If you respect your daughter (and her mother) then she will insist on other males doing the same. If you put her down, she may allow other males to do so too, thinking this is normal. Being respectful is usually as simple as extending normal courtesy. For example, you can respect your daughter's developing need for privacy by asking permission to enter her room when she is in there.

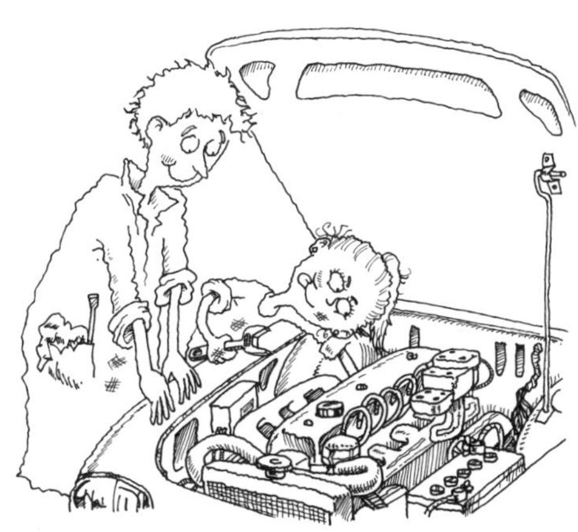

WHEN A CHILD IS DISABLED

In all of my books on family life, it's been a concern to me that I have nothing to say about parenting disabled children. Yet every time I go on tour, parents of babies with all kinds of difficulties come along for some possible assistance. Children with disabilities are part of the family and the community, and deserve to be included. As much as anyone else, they are a plus in all our lives.

I've always felt constrained through lack of personal experience. So I was delighted when I found a beautiful article in the Melbourne *Age* by a mother of a daughter who is severely intellectually disabled, and who can write about her child's life so far with real insight.

Mary Burbridge would be the first to say that her family life has had as many ups and downs as any other. However, it's clear to me that she has triumphed in all kinds of ways and that this would be the kind of message that other parents would like to hear. It is also an example of a very special relationship between a mother and her daughter.

My daughter, my for-ever baby

I have a darling baby. A patient, placid baby who nuzzles warmly into her sheepskin and gives me a sleepy smile when I come in. She sits up, bounces happily and reaches up for a cuddle. I lift her out of bed, and with both hands held she walks unsteadily to the bathroom to have her nappy changed.

She's at a delightful stage, liking to help with dressing and undressing, wanting to hold the spoon but making an awful mess, moving along on the furniture and pulling down whatever she can reach. She loves music – songs and rhymes sung to her, banging on the piano, clapping and finger games, and the neverending, pull-the-string music boxes. She enjoys being taken for walks on sunny days, snatching heads off flowers as we pass, and she would splash and laugh for ever in a warm bath or pool.

I've had my darling baby for nearly twenty years now, and, unless something happens, I guess I'll have her for another twenty years. She's been at the lovely seven- to nine-month stage for a long time, so I don't expect much change.

She still has a sweet baby face, innocent, unmarred by loss or disappointment or anger, and she still has her mass of blonde curls. But her hormones are those of a young woman – a plump, buxom, almost voluptuous young woman – and acne spoils her pretty face. Her hair, though darker now, is still her finest feature. How often I've had cause to be thankful for those lovely curls! People are usually uncomfortable, stuck for something to say, on first meeting my big baby, but they can always say, 'What beautiful hair!' And they do. It helps.

Others I know have a much harder lot with their 'for-ever' babies. Endless years with a fretful, crying child, every mealtime a turmoil of spitting resistance, all activity a cause of spasms and distress. Or a child with full mobility but never learning to heed 'no' or 'stop'; on the go all day every day, getting bigger and stronger with every year, being influenced by powerful adolescent hormones. And without the redeeming beautiful curls.

We met at a special playgroup, a group of young mothers coming to terms with the realization that our children were severely disabled. We talked through our guilt, our grief and disappointment, our anger, as we helped our babies to play, and we've kept in touch. Caring for a severely handicapped child is a big task, as is caring for a baby, but when supports are available it is not all-consuming.

We have had other children and been active in their lives, we've had part-time jobs while the children are in day care, our marriages have survived and we've had family holidays.

And we've become involved in 'the field', working to ensure that the best possible services and supports are available for our children, and for other disabled people and their carers.

School councils, accommodation committees, fund-raising and fetes, lobbying politicians, demonstrations and protests, and self-education – we've done it all, learning as we go. As our children reach nominal adulthood, there are further decisions to be made, battles to be won. We need to be sure that there are suitable day activities available for them when the school system is no longer an option, and that appropriate long-term accommodation will be provided when the time is right for them to leave our care.

For the most part, I've found people sensitive and helpful. Services and supports have been available when I have needed them, and the years have rolled by pretty smoothly.

But there have been jolts and hurts along the way. There was the ideologically pure occupational therapist, who removed my daughter's toys and music box from her wheelchair because they were 'age-inappropriate'. (I responded by tying a book, a chess set and a rock-music tape to her tray, and she banged and chewed them into oblivion.) Or the brutally honest doctor at the children's hospital who said, when I rushed her to casualty with croup, 'I can admit her if you like, but she'd be better off at home. Children like that don't get the best treatment here'. And the bastard who publicly queried my use of a disabled parking sticker (before the rules changed).

Dilemmas arise in the decisions I need to make on my daughter's behalf. As she reached puberty, I was offered, and accepted with misgivings, a hormone injection to stop her having periods. I think I secretly hoped it would stop her body from maturing: that I would be able to pretend for ever that she was still a child. But it didn't, and after a year or so I stopped the injections.

'Why should she wear a bra?' I wondered, until physical size provided an obvious answer. 'What clothes should she wear?' I tend to dress her for her comfort and my convenience, but is this undermining her dignity as a young adult, denigrating her worth as a person? Should I dress her in the sort of things her sister wears; make an outlandish fashion statement on her behalf? What would she choose for herself if she could choose, and does it matter, since she has no concept of fashion or dignity? (These are issues one is made uncomfortably aware of, when working in the broader disability field.)

In deciding to seek an operation to stop her menstruating, was I motivated by her best interests or mine? (The social welfare authorities accepted that it would be in her best interests. Such important decisions are not made by carers alone.)

In years past, children such as ours would very likely have been placed in institutions at an early age. Parents of babies with much lesser disabilities were often advised not to take them home. 'Put her in a home and forget you ever had her,' they were told. And many did.

Recently I spent some time at a large institution, holding meetings with disabled people, their parents and their carers, and I observed a most amazing and moving phenomenon. The residents were in their thirties and had lived in the institution for more than twenty years. The staff were in daily contact with them and met all their physical needs. The parents visited from time to time. Yet, repeatedly, I was struck by the strength and durability of the emotional bond they had with their parents.

They couldn't get close enough, couldn't take their eyes off them, couldn't bear for the parent's attention to be anywhere but on them. An ungainly, non-verbal woman manoeuvred laboriously along the table and sat on her father's knee, pressing her face to his. I felt so sad that these people had not been offered the encouragement and support to keep their child at home for longer; to make the most of the love that was so obviously shared.

These days, fewer disabled children are born. Preventive immunization, genetic counselling and improved obstetric care have contributed to this. Special tests early in pregnancy can identify many malformations or abnormalities, and parents can choose to have the pregnancy terminated. While very few people would choose to bring a severely disabled child into the world if they could avoid it, the implications of this newly acquired capacity to engineer a largely disability-free society need to be examined.

What message does it give to disabled members of our community about their worth, their right to exist and be supported? Will society refuse support for those families who knowingly give birth to a disabled child? Will even minor defects be eliminated, until only perfection is tolerated? And what will this mean for those whose disabilities or deformities could not be predicted, or are acquired after birth?

A friend of mine recently had tests early in her pregnancy, because in her first pregnancy the baby had been found to have a severe foetal defect, necessitating termination, and there was a chance this could recur. She was told these tests showed a different problem, Down's syndrome, and that arrangements had been made for her to have a termination two days later.

She was offered no counselling about what having a child with Down's syndrome would mean, or what factors she would need to consider in making her decision. It was not even appreciated that she had a decision to make! In fact, it was a very difficult decision for her, and only after a lot of heartbreak did she accept that she really could not manage a disabled child in her situation. The attitude to disability shown by her doctors is a little disturbing.

So. What am I saying in all this? There will always be children born with disabilities. And if it happens to you, it's not the end of the world – for you or your baby. No one can predict with certainty what path any child's development will follow. Or what sort of life he or she will be able to lead.

It will not be the life you dreamt about when you were expecting your baby, but it is his or her life. Having a disabled child makes you think about life: what it's for; what's important. And your ideas change quite a lot.

Your life won't be the one you were dreaming about either, but it will be a full life, a rich life. And it could have a lot of joy.

7

Family liberation

At the end of a book that has covered so much ground, I want to share a vision with you. It involves the big picture beyond our homes, but it applies to everything that happens within them. Something new is starting to happen in the world of the family – something that means we can begin to change the world we live in, without leaving our own neighbourhoods to do it.

Time for change Parents have never had a real political voice – perhaps we're just too busy with little children to find the energy. It's as much as some of us can manage to crawl down to a voting booth every five years. But all this is starting to change at express-train speed.

PARENTS ARE ANGRY

Having left the care of our world to politicians and technocrats, what have we ended up with?

Our world is so *polluted* that we sustain genetic damage, and have soaring rates of miscarriage and infertility. Asthma, a problem highly related to air quality, is now a problem for one in every five British children. Likewise with allergies and reactions to the chemical environment. Even the sunshine has become a danger.

Our world is *violent* because of inequity, and crushed families, and a media that promotes violence as a way of life.

Our *economy* is unable to give meaningful or satisfying employment to our men or our teenagers, but it will employ our young mothers, as long as they don't mind what kind of work they do or how poorly they are paid.

When it comes to politics – the 'leadership' of our country – we want a better choice.

When it comes to politics, people are wanting a new priority – that puts people and community first and is not ruled by economic rationalism, yuppie values or earning power as the only measure of human worth.

A POSITIVE NEW ALLIANCE

When there is so little choice and so much frustration, then a new alternative always emerges. In this case, it draws support (surprisingly) from both sides of the philosophical fence. An amazing new alliance is appearing in your neighbourhood – between stereotyped groups such as the alternative lifestyle, high-tech, soft green people, and the right-wing, family-oriented, Christian traditionalists.

This is leading to all kinds of beautiful break-outs from the old stereotypes. When I give lecture tours around Australia, I am meeting at the same gatherings highly responsible, monogamous and hard-working 'hippies' – side by side with straight-backed churchgoers who hug their children, renounce smacking, belong to Amnesty International and boycott Nestlé!

The way forward

I believe that more and more parents are working positively towards a world that embraces serenity, compassion, free-spiritedness and happiness.

In fact, I don't think it is too optimistic to say that a kind of parent power is emerging. It will include and be merged with the green movement, because parents and children are natural environmentalists. It will embrace both feminism and the men's movement, because parents want a good future for both boys and girls, and it will support moves to advance gender relationships. It will make a huge difference to the shape of the twenty-first century.

So, to end this book, here is a suggested manifesto.

A STATEMENT OF BELIEFS TO GUIDE ACTIONS IN FAMILY LIBERATION

- Nothing is more important than raising healthy, happy children.
- No one can or should raise children alone. We all need each other's help.
- In particular we need a society that takes parents' needs very seriously, and funds those needs, in return for the gift we give back of healthy, contributing adults.
- The best way to make children safe is to take more care of parents.
- The best way to deprogramme our overscheduled children is to deprogramme ourselves.
- Parents are responsible to their children – for not smoking around them, for fastening their seat belts, for protecting them from abuse. Kids are not property.
- We must work at allowing children to hang on to childhood as long as possible.
- We must work to increase the positive contact between children and adults. This means abandoning smacking, and fighting sexual abuse, but it also means showing people better ways of connecting with their kids.
- We have to become active mentors to younger people, helping young parents, caring for other people's children, so as to spread the load of raising our young from the overburdened nuclear family into something we haven't had for a long time – real community.
- We have to have family-friendly workplaces, guaranteed by legislation, where fathers and mothers can fit work around their families' needs, instead of having to choose between career and family.
- The concept of family must be broadened to include everyone – single, gay, childless, divorced, elderly, criminal, refugee, businessman, homeless teenager.

We have to put our arms around everyone and say, 'Welcome home!'

A story to end with

A good friend of mine told me this story about an everyday incident at his house, which kind of sums up the whole parenting business. It's about being human and making mistakes and how, as we don't quit, things have a way of working out.

My friend had had a bad day at work. He was tired, it was hot, the house was a mess. It was getting late in the evening.

His oldest boy, a largish thirteen-year-old, was crowding around in the kitchen in that way that teenage boys seem to, kind of taking up all the space at once. Some little argument flared up. The father suddenly found himself yelling, 'Look, just get out of here. Go to your room. I'm sick of you!'

The boy stormed off to his room. Within seconds, the father felt ashamed. He had seen the boy's face as he yelled, seen his eyelids flinch at the violence of his father's anger. He realised the boy would have been physically afraid at that moment.

He tried to figure out why he had been so angry. It didn't fit the situation. Perhaps it was just the day. Either way, the feeling of shame didn't go away.

After a few minutes, he went up to the boy's bedroom, and said sorry. 'I shouldn't have yelled at you. You were hassling me, but it didn't deserve me shouting or sending you away. I'm sorry and I'd like to ask your forgiveness.'

Ouch! It takes guts to do this, it really hurts even just to write this. The boy was very noncommittal. His feelings were hurt, a few words saying 'sorry' were hard to trust. The father went downstairs and cleaned up the kitchen.

After twenty minutes or so, he went up to go to bed. He was in the bathroom brushing his teeth when the son ambled past on his way to the toilet. The youngster had a twinkle in his eye, and spoke softly, but very clearly, as he walked through – 'How come it's so hard to hate you?'

You put a lot in with your kids, from the sleepless nights and the frightening trips to the casualty department, through to homework assignments and a million miles of taxi-driving.

The great thing is that everything you put in counts, and with a bit of luck, one day they will realise it. Love adds up to something. Nothing else matters half as much.

Postscript

Only caring parents bother to read books about parenting. You will find, from reading this book, that some parts 'hit home' immediately, and others were not so relevant or even interesting.

Probably you skipped parts and read others. Good, because the book was designed to be used in just that way. The parts that have seemed to fit your situation and apply to your kids will have set you thinking after you put the book down, and even sometimes you may have found you were saying different things or feeling easier or less uptight as you dealt with your children.

That's how change happens. You can make a deliberate effort if you want to, but you can't help but improve your skill as a parent as these ideas come together with all your other thoughts and learning.

Sometimes you may go back to reread parts of the book and find things that you didn't notice at first – because you have progressed since the first time and can take in more. You might use the book when you get depressed or feel stuck, to help you unstick.

You will find that you think about how to use 'I' messages instead of using hypnotic put-downs when talking to your kids You may think more about affection and positive attention. Or it might be active listening that really helps you get closer to your kids. Assertiveness may be the new you! Or you may be working on getting your family into the shape you want it to be.

Sometimes you'll feel like nothing has changed – it all seems too difficult. And then another day you'll realise that you, and your kids, and the people around you, are much, much happier than before. Real progress comes in like the tide, in waves. Learn to trust it.

Appendix

If you've enjoyed this book, here are some others that deal with kids and parents. You might find them useful.

Suggested Reading

James & Jongeward. *Born to Win*, Addison-Wesley, Reading, Mass., 1996

Liedloff, Jean. *The Continuum Concept*, Penguin, London, 1989

Axline, Virginia. *Dibs*, Penguin, London, 1990

Lindenfield, Gael. *Confident Children*, Thorsons, London, 1996

Further information (for those who work with children)

The thesis of this book is simple – that children grow and develop the way they do, largely as a result of what we say to them, and the way we say it. The way that children are thus programmed is covered in the first chapter. The most startling piece of information, well known to clinicians but little known amongst the general public, is the degree to which programming takes place hypnotically – out of the awareness of either children or parents.

My goal in writing the book is to help parents recognise and eliminate what I call 'put-down parenting' – the use of destructive messages as a form of child control. All the chapters following the first are there to provide alternatives to the put-down style, so that parents may relinquish it and not be left at a loss for what to do instead.

Childcare and counselling professionals may recognise many of the concepts used in this book, however for those wishing to trace particular ideas to their source, or to explore the implications for helping families and children, a brief summary of sources for each chapter follows:

1. Seeds in the mind

The significance of childhood 'taping' of parental messages was first recognised by Eric Berne, and is a central part of the treatment system known as Transactional Analysis. Robert and Mary Goulding systematise the negative programming of children into ten basic 'don't' messages, and found that it was not passive programming (as Berne had believed), but an 'out-of-awareness' co-operation by the child that allowed the messages to remain in action, often severely impairing adult life chances. Tracing and bringing into awareness this programming forms a very powerful treatment technique known as 'Redecision Therapy'.

Children who have been severely deprived and/or disturbed may lack replacement messages even if placed in a caring environment. Jacqui and Aaraon Schiff demonstrated success with a system of intensive reprogramming of such children, with highly directive and highly nurturant components, known as Reparenting.

The concept of 'accidental hypnosis' is directly attributable to the work of Milton Erikson, and is described both in his own books and the many books written about him since his death. In particular, Richard Bandler and John Grinder have made clear how this process takes place and also how it can be deliberately used. The ethics of this are currently being debated.

'You-messages' were popularised under that name by Thomas Gordon, in the immediately successful Parent Effectiveness system. Under the name of 'attributions' they are discussed in almost any Family Therapy text, for instance books by Virginia Satir, Jay Haley, R. D. Laing, etc.

2. What children really want

The early works of Rene Spitz, John Bowlby and others, and writing on the conditions known as hospitalism and marasmus led to the concept of 'positive strokes'. The whole behaviour modification approach builds on this concept – that 'what you stroke is what you get'. The work of Amelia Auckett on baby massage is a good introduction to affectionate parenting.

3. Curing by listening

Or 'Active Listening', evolved from Carl Rogers' client-centred counselling, as applied to everyday situations. Once again Thomas Gordon takes credit for making this approach available to parents.

4. Kids and emotions

Emotions are best understood as variants of the four biological states – anger, fear, sadness, joy. While these are innate, the expression of them is shaped by familial and cultural factors to an enormous degree. Counselling theory and practice – and the work of Harvey Jackins – is helpful in understanding and freeing up the emotional side of being human. The systematic teaching of expressive and yet socially constructive emotional responses was developed by the Reparenting school of Transactional Analysis. The concept of 'racket' or phoney emotions aimed at controlling others, is an important one. Tantrums, shyness, and sulking or boredom are very common childhood disturbances of emotion which are tolerated too much in our culture, and so often continue into adult behaviour – as violence, depression, and so on. Ken and Elizabeth Mellor first taught us about the false nature of shyness, and how to 'cure' it.

5. The assertive parent

Assertiveness is widely known and taught, but not often applied directly to parenting. This is a pity because if parents were assertive, they would not need to use put-downs. Adequate books and courses on assertiveness deal with the surface skills, the really useful books and courses help parents look at their own negative programming.

The 'Tough Love' movement in the US looks very worthwhile for parents with problem kids.

6. Family shape

Margaret Mead, in her irrepressible way, did most to remind us that we no longer live in real families, but in fragments of families. More elaborated ways to look at intrafamily structure are taught by Virginia Satir, Margaret Topham, Sal Minuchin, or any 'structural family therapy' source.

7. Ages and stages

The development stages used in this book were based on the work of Pamela Levin. Jean Illsley-Clarke's book *Self-Esteem: A Family Affair* (no longer in print) which expands Levin's ideas further, is the most useful and down-to-earth child development book that I have read – ever.

8. Energy and how to save it

The view that energy can be moved between people is scientifically far from respectable, and there has been little documentation. The experience, on the other hand, of being 'drained' by some people, and of giving and receiving energy to and from others, is almost universally acknowledged by parents. The work of Ken Mellor in Australia, and Julie Henderson and other 'bioenergeticists' in the US point to this being more than just a metaphor, and can be lifesaving for those parents for whom exhaustion is a daily hazard.

Resources

The Mother and Baby Book by Shaaron Biddulph (available from Parent Network; tel. 0171 735 1214) is a beautiful and detailed guide to the craft of loving and educating babies through to preschool age. It is a book that only a woman could write.

Children's Relaxation Tape by Madhu Lilley is one of the most beautiful aids for children to relaxing and falling asleep with positive and strengthening imagery. Of the many beneficial relaxation tapes, this simple one is the favourite of our children. Available from Parent Network, tel. as above.

Parents and *Practical Parenting* magazines, as well as the publications of the National Childbirth Trust and National Breastfeeding Alliance, all have good, critical and consumer conscious news and views on parenthood and are good value.

The most progressive and non-commercial publication in the world that we have found is *Mothering* magazine, available from PO Box 532 Mt Morris, Illinois 61054, USA. We find this a great source of inspiration.

On the subjects of fathering and of raising boys, Steve's book *Manhood* is published by Hawthorne Press. On marriage and couple relationships, Steve and Shaaron's book, *The Making of Love*, is available from Parent Network; tel. as above.

Acknowledgements

I am profoundly indebted to Shaaron Biddulph for her skill with children, and the balance she brings to my masculine way of writing. Shaaron conceived of the sections on childcare damage and 'our home is a no smacking zone'. She refined the use of 'stand and think' and 'dealing' as applied to young children, and has taught these ideas to hundreds of parents. Our son and daughter learned with us. And, as with every family, hundreds of people helped.

Many thanks to Paul Stanish for drawing the cartoons, and Steve Miller for the beautiful cover design. And especial thanks to Wanda Whiteley, Charlotte Ridings, Paul Redhead and Megan Slyfield at Thorsons UK for believing in our books and bringing them to that sceptred isle.

Thanks to Boxtree Limited for permission to quote from *Are Mothers Really Necessary?* by Bob Mullen; Rosie Lever for permission to quote from *Such Sweet Sorrow*; Christopher Green for permission to quote from *Toddler Taming*; *Readers Digest* magazine for permission to quote from Karl Zinmeister's article, 'Hard Truths about Day Care'; the Australian Institute of Family Studies, especially Gay Ochiltree for her book, *Children in Australian Families*; the Melbourne *Age* and Mary Burbridge for permission to use in full her article, 'My Daughter, My Forever Baby'; the Melbourne *Age* for permission to use an excerpt from their editorial on parent pay; the *Mercury*, Hobart, for permission to reproduce the Benjamin Spock quote and the material on working mothers; the library staff at the Institute for Early Childhood Development at Kew, Melbourne, for their help and research facilities.

Experts can be a hazard to your family's health.
Luckily, this is a non-expert book!
Please take it for what it is – friendly suggestions,
and support for your own good sense.

In your heart,
YOU know what's right
for you and your children.

Parent Network

Would you like support for carrying out some of the ideas in this book?

Then you might be interested in attending a course run by Parent Network to help break old patterns and give new strategies for handling the ups and downs of family life

Parent Network is a national charity founded in 1986 which trains parents to run courses for other parents. Courses include *Parent-Link*, *Understanding Children*, *Understanding Adolescents* and *Conflict Management Between Children.*

Parents, grandparents and carers from all kinds of backgrounds, cultures and ethnic groups are welcomed.

Our philosophy

Parent Network believes that parenting is the most important job most of us will ever do. Every child and every parent is unique so parenting must be an art rather than a science – and like artists we as parents are constantly learning and can gain from looking at how others do things.

Love is an active verb – a 'doing word' – putting the feeling into practice in the day-to-day round of keeping a family going is hard. Our own children 'wind us up' in ways which we could not have imagined before we had them. Parent Network courses help us to clarify our feelings about how we were brought up – the good things as well as what we disliked. Remembering our own childhoods helps us to understand and empathise with our children.

Our style and approach to running courses is based on ideas of helping everyone to join in, our facilitators are parents themselves and share their own experiences – what worked for them, and what didn't! They also teach skills in listening and assertiveness which help to build relationships and encourage responsibility in children.

How to find us

Write to us or phone the number below and you will be given details of your local contact:

Parent Network
Winchester House
Kennington Park
11 Cranmer Road
London SW9 6EJ
Tel: 020 7 735
Helpline: 020 7735 1214 (10am–4pm weekdays)
Fax: 020 7735 4692
E-mail: info@parentnetwork.demon.co.uk

Raising Boys

Why Boys are Different – and How to Help Them Become Happy and Well-Balanced Men

Steve Biddulph

Boys need to be parented in a different way from girls with their own very special psychological and physical make-up. Home, society and education have failed boys badly – and these failures lead to unhappy men who cannot fully become happy, responsible, emotionally-confident adults.

It is essential that boys spend more time learning about manhood from their fathers. And through the teen years a boy ideally needs a male mentor outside his immediate family to teach him the best way to live. Without these things boys can turn to alcohol, drugs and despair and fail to grow up into feeling, responsible adults.

A book which gives good advice on: the stages of boyhood; how a mother teaches about life and love; how schools need to change to be made a good place for boys; testosterone and how it changes behaviour; how to be a good father; how to teach boys to have a caring attitude to girls and about sex.

How Love Works

How to stay in love as a couple and true to yourself even with kids

Steve Biddulph and Shaaron Biddulph

In the tradition of 'Families and How to Survive them' and Relate's successful relationships guides, but with a difference: this is a humourous, loving guide to creating a successful long-term relationship in Biddulph's popular and very readable style.

Includes:
- Compatability and commitment
- Making of Love – keeping the romance long term even after the third wake-up call that night
- Arguments do happen
- Sex and tenderness
- Happy couple = happy children